Hooked on Style

Hooked on Style

CATHERINE N. BLYTHE

and Patons Design Studio

sixth&spring books

New York

sixth&spring
books

EDITORIAL DIRECTOR
Trisha Malcolm

ART DIRECTORS
Lydia Ricci and Sara Scanlan

BOOK DIVISION MANAGER
Erica Smith

PRODUCTION MANAGER
David Joinnides

PHOTOGRAPHY
Jurek Wyszynski © 2005

PRESIDENT, SIXTH&SPRING BOOKS
Art Joinnides

PATONS DESIGN TEAM:

DESIGNERS
Svetlana Avraka
Zena Low
Kara Guild
Gayle Bunn
Fiona Ellis

MARKETING MANAGER
Sara Arblaster

GRAPHICS:
Julie Le

MARKETING SUPPORT
Doris Erb
Kathy Hicks
Barb Ward
Leianne Gooding

CREATIVE AND MARKETING DIRECTOR
Catherine N. Blythe

Library of Congress Control Number: 2005929983
ISBN: 1-931543-81-X
ISBN-13: 978-1-931543-81-1

Manufactured in China
1 3 5 7 9 10 8 6 4 2
First Edition

Contents

INTRODUCTION 7

INSTRUCTIONS 8

ENSEMBLES 13

ACCESSORIES 43

ELEGANCE 87

SPRING GLAMOUR 117

RESOURCES 175

ACKNOWLEDGMENTS 176

Introduction

For those who crochet, there is nothing more satisfying than taking yarn and a hook and creating a garment that is truly unique. Whether one crochets to make gifts or simply to soothe one's own soul, this age-old craft has become new again, with trendy crocheted garments and accessories showing up on fashion show runways around the world. The design team at Patons has a special passion for crochet and we are proud to present this inspired collection of over 25 of our most cherished crochet patterns. From the simplicity of chic scarves, to the delicacy of lace work wraps, to the hippest of accessories and garments, this ultimate crochet book—with all designs featuring Patons exceptional yarns—takes crochet to a new level of beauty, sophistication, and fun!

Both beginners and experts will find themselves inspired by not only the intriguing and fashion forward designs, but also by the excellence and quality of Patons' renowned pattern writing. The undeniably talented designers at Patons—Svetlana Avrakh, Zena Low, Kara Guild and Gayle Bunn, along with Sara Arblaster, Julie Le and Doris Erb—contribute to the glorious transformation of balls of the finest yarn into dynamic designs and imagery. Their vision and passion for the craft is apparent in each and every detail.

There is so much to choose from in this creative collection that this book is sure to become your inspirational resource for the best in crochet designs. So settle in with your favourite Patons yarn, your favourite crochet hook (worn smooth with use) and any one of these delightful designs, and enjoy creating your own piece of magic.

Happy Crocheting!

Catherine N. Blythe

Learn to Crochet
INSTRUCTIONS

SLIP KNOT

1 Make a loop, then hook another loop through it.

2 Tighten gently and slide the knot up to the hook.

CHAIN STITCH (ch)

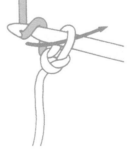

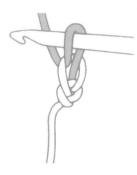

1 Yarn over hook (yoh) and draw the yarn through to form a new loop without tightening up the previous one.

2 Repeat to form as many chains (ch) as required. Do not count the slip knot as a stitch.

SLIP STITCH (sl st)

This is the shortest crochet stitch and unlike other stitches is not used on its own to produce a fabric. It is used for joining, shaping and where necessary carrying the yarn to another part of the fabric for the next stage.

Insert hook into work (second chain from hook), yarn over hook (yoh) and draw the yarn through both the work and loop on hook in one movement.

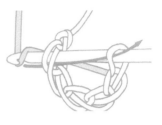

To join a chain ring with a slip stitch (sl st), insert hook into first chain (ch), yarn over hook (yoh) and draw through both the work and the yarn on hook in one movement.

SINGLE CROCHET (sc)

1 Insert the hook into the work (2nd chain (ch) from hook on starting chain), *yarn over hook (yoh) and draw yarn through the work only.

2 Yarn over hook (yoh) again and draw the yarn through both loops on the hook.

3 1 single crochet (sc) made. Insert hook into next stitch: repeat (rep) from * in step 1.

HALF DOUBLE CROCHET (hdc)

1 Yarn over hook (yoh) and insert the hook into the work (3rd chain (ch) from hook on starting chain).

2 *Yarn over hook (yoh) and draw through the work only.

3 Yarn over hook (yoh) again and draw through all three loops on the hook.

4 1 hdc made. Yarn over hook (yoh), insert hook into next stitch (st); repeat (rep) from step 2.

DOUBLE CROCHET (dc)

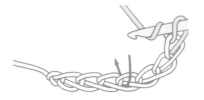  

1 Yarn over hook (yoh) and insert the hook into the work (4th chain from hook on starting chain).

2 *Yarn over hook (yoh) and draw through the work only.

3 Yarn over hook (yoh) and draw through the first two loops only.

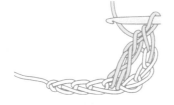

4 Yarn over hook (yoh) and draw through the last two loops on the hook.

5 1 dc made. Yarn over hook (yoh), insert hook into next stitch (st), repeat (rep) from step 2.

Ensembles

Bikini

SIZES

Top: To fit bra cup sizes A, B or C.

Bottom: One Size

MATERIALS

Patons Grace (50 g/1.75 oz)

Size	A	B	C	
Top: (60604 Terracotta)	1	1	2	**ball(s)**
Bottom (one size): (60604 Terracotta)			2	**balls**

Size 2.25 mm (U.S. B or 1) crochet hook **or size needed to obtain tension.** Invisible elastic thread for Bottom.

TENSION

24 sc and 28 rows = 4 ins [10 cm]

INSTRUCTIONS

The instructions are written for smallest size. If changes are necessary for larger sizes the instructions will be written thus ( ).

TOP

Cup (make 2). Ch 15 (**16**-20).

1st row: (RS). 1 sc in 2nd ch from hook. 1 sc in each ch to last ch. 5 sc in last ch. Mark center sc. **Do not turn.** Working into other side of ch, work 1 sc in each rem loop of ch to end of ch. Turn. 31 (**33**-41) sc.

2nd row: Ch 1. 1 sc in each sc to end of row. Turn.

3rd row: Ch 1. 1 sc in each sc to center sc. 5 (**5**-3) sc in center sc. 1 sc in each sc to end of row. Turn.

4th row: As 2nd row.

5th row: Ch 1. 1 sc in each sc to center sc. 3 sc in center sc. 1 sc in each sc to end of row. Turn. Rep last 4 rows 4 (**5**-6) times more, then 2nd row once. 61 (**69**-69) sc.

All sizes: Next row: (WS). 1 sc in each of next 3 (**4**-4) sc. *Ch 1. Miss next sc. 1 sc in each of next 2 sc. Rep from * to last 1 (**2**-2) sc. 1 sc in each of last 1 (**2**-2) sc. Turn.

Next row: Ch 1. 1 sc in each of first 1 (**2**-2) sc. *5 dc in next ch-1 sp. 1 sc in next ch-1 sp. Rep from * to last 3 (**4**-4) sc. 1 sc in each of last 3 (**4**-4) sc. Fasten off.

Join Cups and Make Ties: Ch 95. With WS of work facing, work 28 (**28**-30) sc evenly across bottom of first Cup. Ch 4. Work 28 (**28**-30) sc evenly across bottom of second Cup. Ch 96. Turn.

Next row: (RS). 1 sl st in 2nd ch from hook. 1 sl st in each of next 94 ch. 1 sc in each of next 28 (**28**-30) sc. 1 sc in each of next 4 ch. 1 sc in each of next 28 (**28**-30) sl st. 1 ss in each of next 95 ch. Fasten off.

Neck Ties: With RS of work facing, join yarn with sl st to top center 5 dc group. Ch 106. 1 sl st in 2nd ch from hook. 1 sl st in each ch to end of ch. Fasten off. Rep for Second Cup.

BOTTOM

Back: Ch 63.

1st row: 1 sc in 2nd ch from hook. 1 sc in each ch to end of ch. 62 sc. Turn.

2nd row: Ch 1. 1 sc in each sc to end of row. Turn. Rep last row 7 times more.

Back shaping: 1st row: (RS). Draw up a loop in each of first 2 sts. *Yoh and draw through all loops on hook* – sc2tog made. 1 sc in each sc to last 2 sc. Sc2tog over last 2 sc. Turn.

2nd row: Ch 1. 1 sc in first st. 1 sc in each st to end of row.

Rep last 2 rows until there are 14 sc, ending with RS facing for next row.

Next row: Ch 1. 1 sc in each sc to end of row. Turn.

Rep last row 19 times more.

Front shaping: Next row: Ch 1. 2 sc in first st. 1 sc in each st to last st. 2 sc in last st. Turn.

Next 2 rows: Ch 1. 1 sc in each st to end of row. Turn.

Rep last 3 rows 13 times more. Fasten off.

Back Edging and Side Ties: 1st row: Ch 55. With RS of work facing, sl st in first ch of foundation ch on Back. Ch 1. 1 sc in each ch of foundation ch. Ch 56. Turn.

2nd row: 1 sl st in 2nd ch from hook. 1 ss in each of next 54 ch. 1 sc in each sc across Back. 1 sl st in each of next 55 ch. Fasten off.

Rep for Front Edging and Side Ties.

Leg Edging: 1st row: With RS of work facing, join yarn with sl st to Front Side edge where Tie is joined. Ch 1. Work 1 row sc evenly along Leg Opening. Turn.

2nd row: Ch 1. 1 sc in each sc to end of row. Fasten off.

Rep for second Leg Edging joining yarn with sl st to Back Side edge where tie is joined.

Thread invisible elastic through last sc row of Back, Front and Leg Edgings.

Mesh Tunic

SIZES

Bust measurement:

Small	30-32	ins	[76-81	cm]	
Medium	34-36	"	[86-91	"	]
Large	38-40	"	[97-102	"	]

Finished bust:

Small	38	ins	[97	cm]	
Medium	42	"	[107	"	]
Large	46	"	[117	"	]

MATERIALS

Patons Grace (50 g/1.75 oz)

Size	S	M	L
(60603 Apricot)	9	10	11 **balls**

Size 3.25 mm (U.S. D or 3) crochet hook **or size needed to obtain tension.**

TENSION

21 dc and 10 rows = 4 ins [10 cm]

INSTRUCTIONS

The instructions are written for smallest size. If changes are necessary for larger sizes the instructions will be written thus ( ).

BACK AND FRONT (make alike)

Ch 114 (**130**-154).

1st row: (RS). 1 sc in 2nd ch from hook. (Ch 4. Miss next 3 ch. 1 sc in next ch) 8 (**10**-12) times. Miss next 3 ch. *(3 dc. Ch 1. 3 dc)* all in next ch - shell made. Miss next 3 ch. 1 sc in next sc. (Ch 4. Miss next 3 ch. 1 sc in next ch) 8 (**8**-10) times. Miss next 3 ch. Shell in next ch. Miss next 3 ch. 1 sc in next ch. (Ch 4. Miss next 3 ch. 1 sc in next ch) 8 (**10**-12) times. Turn.

2nd row: Ch 5. 1 sc in first ch-4 sp. (Ch 4. 1 sc in next ch-4 sp) 7 (**9**-11) times. Ch 2. Shell in top of next shell. Ch 2. (1 sc in next ch-4 sp. Ch 4) 7 (**7**-9) times. 1 sc in next ch-4 sp. Ch 2. Shell in top of next shell. Ch 2. (1 sc in next ch-4 sp. Ch 4) 7 (**9**-11) times. 1 sc in next ch-4 sp. Ch 3. 1 dc in last sc. Turn.

3rd row: Ch 1. 1 sc in first dc. (Ch 4. 1 sc in next ch-4 sp) 7 (**9**-11) times. Ch 4. 1 sc in next ch 2 sp. Shell in top of next shell. 1 sc in next ch 2 sp. (Ch 4. 1 sc in next ch-4 sp) 7 (**7**-9) times. Ch 4. 1 sc in next ch-2 sp. Shell in top of next shell. 1 sc in next ch-2 sp. (Ch 4. 1 sc in next ch-4 sp) 7 (**9**-11) times. Ch 4. 1 sc in 2nd ch of ch 5.

Rep last 2 rows until work from beg measures 24 (**25**-26) ins [61 (**64**-66.5) cm], ending with WS facing for next row.

Next row: Ch 5. 1 sc in first ch-4 sp. (Ch 4. 1 sc in next ch-4 sp) 6 (**8**-10) times. Ch 4. 1 sc in next ch-2 sp. Ch 4. 1 sc in top of next shell. Ch 4. 1 sc in next ch-2 sp. Ch 4. (1 sc in next ch-4 sp. Ch 4) 6 (**6**-8) times. 1 sc in top of next shell. Ch 4. 1 sc in next ch-2 sp. Ch 4. (1 sc in next ch-4 sp. Ch 4) 7 (**9**-11) times. 1 sc in next ch-4 sp. Ch 2. 1 dc in last sc. Turn.

Next row: Ch 1. 1 sc in first dc. 1 sc in next ch -2 sp. *Ch 1. Miss next sc. 3 sc in next ch-4 sp. Rep from * to last sc and turning ch 5. Ch 1. Miss last sc. 1 sc in ch-5 sp.

Next row: Ch 1. 1 sc in first sc. *Shell in next ch-1 sp. 1 sc in next ch-1 sp. Rep from * to end of row. Fasten off.

SLEEVES

Ch 74 (**82**-82).

1st row: (RS). 1 sc in 2nd ch from hook. (Ch 4. Miss next 3 ch. 1 sc in next ch) 8 (**9**-9) times. Miss next 3 ch. Shell in next ch. Miss next 3 ch. 1 sc in next ch. (Ch 4. Miss next 3 ch. 1 sc in next ch) 8 (**9**-9) times. Turn.

2nd row: Ch 5. 1 sc in first ch-4 sp. (Ch 4. 1 sc in next ch-4 sp) 7 (**8**-8) times. Ch 2. Shell in top of next shell. Ch 2. (1 sc in next ch-4 sp. Ch 4) 7 (**8**-8) times. 1 sc in next ch-4 sp. Ch 3. 1 dc in last sc. Turn.

3rd row: Ch 1. 1 sc in first dc. (Ch 4. 1 sc in next ch-4 sp) 7 (**8**-8) times. Ch 4. 1 sc in next ch-2 sp. Shell in top of next shell. 1 sc in next ch-2 sp. (Ch 4. 1 sc in next ch-4 sp) 7 (**8**-8) times. Ch 4. 1 sc in 2nd ch of ch 5. Turn.

Rep last 2 rows until work from beg measures 3 ins [7.5 cm], ending on a 2nd row, thus having RS facing for next row.

Next row: (Increase row). Ch 1. 1 sc in first dc. Ch 3. 1 sc in first ch-3 sp. (Ch 4. 1 sc in next ch-4 sp) 7 (**8**-8) times. Ch 4. 1 sc in next ch-2 sp. Shell in top of next shell. 1 sc in next ch-2 sp. (Ch 4. 1 sc in next ch 4 sp) 7 (**8**-8) times. Ch 4. 1 sc in ch-5 sp. Ch 3. 1 sc in same ch-5 sp. Turn.

Next row: Ch 5. 1 sc in first ch-3 sp. (Ch 4. 1 sc in next ch-4 sp) 8 (**9**-9) times. Ch 2. Shell in top of next shell. Ch 2. (1 sc in next ch-4 sp. Ch 4) 8 (**9**-9) times. 1 sc in ch-3 sp. Ch 3. 1 dc in last sc. Turn.

Next row: Ch 1. 1 sc in first dc. (Ch 4. 1 sc in next ch-4 sp) 8 (**9**-9) times. Ch 4. 1 sc in next ch-2 sp. Shell in top of next shell. 1 sc in next ch-2

sp. (Ch 4. 1 sc in next ch-4 sp) 8 (**9**-9) times. Ch 4. 1 sc in 2nd ch of ch 5. Turn.

Next row: Ch 5. 1 sc in first ch-4 sp. (Ch 4. 1 sc in next ch-4 sp) 8 (**9**-9) times. Ch 2. Shell in top of next shell. Ch 2. (1 sc in next ch-4 sp. Ch 4) 8 (**9**-9) times. 1 sc in next ch-4 sp. Ch 3. 1 dc in last sc. Turn.

Rep last 2 rows until work from beg measures 5 ins [12.5 cm], ending with RS facing for next row.

Next row: (Increase row). Ch 1. 1 sc in first dc. Ch 3. 1 sc in first ch-3 sp. (Ch 4. 1 sc in next ch-4 sp) 8 (**9**-9) times. Ch 4. 1 sc in next ch-2 sp. Shell in top of next shell. 1 sc in next ch-2 sp. (Ch 4. 1 sc in next ch 4 sp) 8 (**9**-9) times. Ch 4. 1 sc in ch-5 sp. Ch 3. 1 sc in same ch-5 sp. Turn.

Next row: Ch 5. 1 sc in first ch-3 sp. (Ch 4. 1 sc in next ch-4 sp) 9 (**10**-10) times. Ch 2. Shell in top of next shell. Ch 2. (1 sc in next ch-4 sp. Ch 4) 9 (**10**-10) times. 1 sc in ch-3 sp. Ch 3. 1 dc in last sc. Turn.

Next row: Ch 1. 1 sc in first dc. (Ch 4. 1 sc in next ch-4 sp) 9 (**10**-10) times. Ch 4. 1 sc in next ch-2 sp. Shell in top of next shell. 1 sc in next ch-2 sp. (Ch 4. 1 sc in next ch-4 sp) 9 (**10**-10) times. Ch 4. 1 sc in 2nd ch of ch 5. Turn.

Next row: Ch 5. 1 sc in first ch-4 sp. (Ch 4. 1 sc in next ch-4 sp) 9 (**10**-10) times. Ch 2. Shell in top of next shell. Ch 2. (1 sc in next ch-4 sp. Ch 4) 9 (**10**-10) times. 1 sc in next ch-4 sp. Ch 3. 1 dc in last sc. Turn.

INSTRUCTIONS CONT.

Cont in pat working incs every 2 ins [5 cm] from previous inc row 4 times more.

Cont even in pat until work from beg measures 18 (**19**-20) ins [45.5 (**48**-51) cm], ending with RS facing for next row. Fasten off.

FINISHING

Pin garment pieces to measurements. Steam lightly and cover with a damp cloth leaving to dry.

Bottom Edging: 1st row: With WS of work facing, join yarn with sl st to first ch of bottom. Ch 1. 1 sc in same sp as last sl st. *3 sc in next ch-3 sp. Ch 1. Miss next sc. Rep from * to last ch-3 sp. 3 sc in last ch-3 sp. 1 sc in last st. Turn.

2nd row: Ch 1. 1 sc in first sc. *Shell in next ch-1 sp. 1 sc in next ch-1 sp. Rep from * to end of row. Fasten off.

Sleeve Edging: Work as given for Bottom Edging.

Joining Shoulders: Place markers on front and back top edges 5 ins [12.5 cm] in from side edges. Place Back and Front with RS facing each other. Join yarn with sl st to top of first shell, working through both thicknesses, 1 sc through top of first shells. *Ch 3. 1 sc through top of next corresponding shells. Rep from * to marker. Fasten off. Rep for other shoulder.

Place markers on front and back side edges 9 (**9½**-9½) ins [23 (**24**-24) cm] down from shoulder seams. Crochet sleeves between markers working through both thicknesses using (1 sc. Ch 1) around armhole. Crochet side and sleeve seams through both thicknesses working (1 sc. Ch 1) along seams.

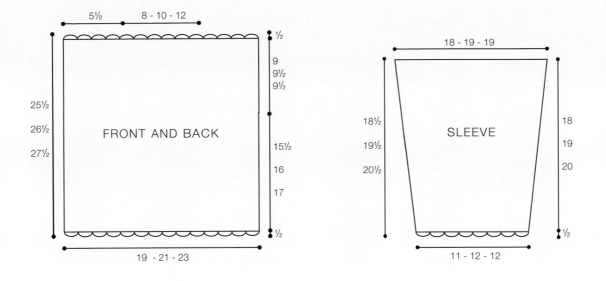

FRONT AND BACK

5½   8 - 10 - 12

½
9
9½
9½

25½
26½
27½

15½
16
17

½

19 - 21 - 23

SLEEVE

18 - 19 - 19

18½
19½
20½

18
19
20

½

11 - 12 - 12

Tote Bag

SIZE

13 ins [33 cm] wide x 15 ins [38 cm] long.

STITCH GLOSSARY

DcCl: *Yoh and insert hook in next ch or st. Yoh and draw up a loop. Yoh and draw through 2 loops on hook.* Miss next ch or st. Rep from * to * in next ch or st. Yoh and draw through all 3 loops on hook.

MATERIALS

Patons Grace (50 g/1.75 oz)

Main Color (MC) (60104 Azure)	1	**ball**
Contrast A (60027 Ginger)	1	**ball**
Contrast B (60005 Snow)	2	**balls**
Contrast C (60409 Ruby)	1	**ball**

Sizes 2.75 mm (U.S. C or 2) and 4.50 mm (U.S. 7) crochet hooks **or size needed to obtain tension**.

TENSION

22 dc and 11 rows = 4 ins [10 cm]

INSTRUCTIONS

Front and Back (make 2 pieces alike)

Center Strip: With smaller hook and A, ch 30.

1st row: Miss 3 ch (counts as 1 dc). Work 1 DcCl inserting hook first in next ch. Ch 1. *Work 1 DcCl inserting hook first in same ch as previous DcCl. Ch 1. Rep from * to end of row. 1 dc in same ch as last DcCl. Turn.

2nd row: Ch 3 (counts as 1 dc). Miss first st. 1 DcCl inserting hook first in next st. Ch 1. *1 DcCl inserting hook first in same st as previous DcCl. Ch 1. Rep from * to end of row. 1 dc in same st as last DcCl. Turn.

Rep 2nd row once more.

Change to B and rep 2nd row 3 times.

Change to MC and rep 2nd row 3 times.

Change to B and rep 2nd row 14 times.

Change to MC and rep 2nd row 3 times.

Change to A and rep 2nd row 3 times. Fasten off.

Top or Bottom Strips: With RS of work facing and smaller hook, join MC with sl st to first st and working across one long edge of Center Strip, proceed as follows:

1st row: Ch 1. 1 sc in same sp as sl st. *2 sc in next dc post. Rep from * to end of row. 1 sc in last st. Turn. 57 sts.

2nd row: Ch 3 (counts as 1 dc). Miss first sc. 1 DcCl inserting hook first in next st. Ch 1. *1 DcCl inserting hook first in same st as previous DcCl. Ch 1. Rep from * to end of row. 1 dc in same st as last DcCl. Turn.

Rep last row in the following stripe sequence:

With MC, work 2 rows.

With B, work 2 rows.

With A, work 3 rows. Fasten off.

Rep across rem long edge of Center Strip.

Join Front and Back: Place WS of Front and Back facing each other. Join A with sl st in top left corner. Ch 1. 1 sc in same sp as sl st. Working through both thicknesses, work 1 row sc evenly down side to bottom. 3 sc in corner st. Work 58 sc along lower edge of bag. 3 sc in corner st. Work 1 row sc evenly up opposite side. Fasten off.

Top Edging: 1st rnd: With smaller hook, join A with sl st to first sc of top edge of Front. Work 1 row sc evenly around. Join with sl st to first sc.

2nd rnd: Working from **left** to right, instead of from **right** to left as usual, work 1 reverse sc in each sc around. Join with sl st to first sc. Fasten off.

Bottom Edging: 1st row: With smaller hook, join C with sl st to first sc of bottom edge. Ch 2. Miss first sc. Work 1 hdc in each of 59 sts along lower edge of bag. Turn.

2nd row: Ch 3. Miss first hdc. *1 dc in next hdc. Ch 1. Miss next st. Rep from * to end of row. Turn.

3rd row: Ch 2. Miss first dc. *1 hdc in next ch-1 sp. 1 hdc in next dc. Rep from * to end of row. Join B. Turn.

4th row: With B, ch 1. 1 sc in first hdc. *(1 sc. Ch 5. 1 sc) in next hdc. 1 sc in each of next 7 hdc. Rep from * to last 2 hdc. (1 sc. Ch 5. 1 sc) in next hdc. 1 sc in last hdc. Turn.

5th row: Ch 1. Miss first st. *(1 hdc. 11 dc. 1 hdc) in ch-5 sp. Miss next st. 1 sc in each of next 5 sts. Rep from * to last ch-5 sp. (1 hdc. 11 dc. 1 hdc) in last ch-5 sp. 1 sc in last st. Join A. Turn.

6th row: *With A, ch 4. Miss next hdc and 3 dc. 1 sc in next st. Ch 3. Sl st in 3rd ch from hook - picot made. Ch 1. Miss next st. 1 sc in next st. Picot. Ch 1. Miss next st. Picot. Ch 4. Miss next 5 sts. 1 sc in next st. Rep from * to end of row. Fasten off.

MEDALLION

With smaller hook and C, ch 5. Join with sl st to first ch to form a ring.

1st rnd: Ch 1. 16 sc in ring. Join with sl st to first sc.

2nd rnd: Ch 1. 1 sc in same sp as last sl st. 1 sc in next sc. *(1 sc. Ch 9. 1 sc) all in next sc.** 1 sc in each of next 3 sc. Rep from * twice more, then rep from * to ** once. 1 sc in next sc. Sl st to first sc.

3rd rnd: Ch 1. 1 sc in same sp as last sl st. *Miss next 2 sc. Work (2 hdc. 17 dc. 2 hdc) all in next 9 ch arch. Miss next 2 sc. 1 sc in next sc. Rep from * 3 times more omitting 1 sc at end of last rep. Sl st to first sc.

4th rnd: Ch 1. Insert hook 2 rnds below in first st (in top of 1st rnd). *Yoh and draw up a loop to height of current row. Yoh and draw through both loops on hook* - long sc made. *Ch 5. Miss next 5 sts. 1 sc in next st. Picot. (Ch 5. Miss next 4 sts. 1 sc in next st. Picot) twice. Ch 5. Miss next 5 sts. 1 long sc 2 rows below over next st. Rep from * 3 times more omitting long sc at end of last rep. Sl st to first long sc. Fasten off. Sew to center Front of Bag as illustrated.

Handles: (make 2). With larger hook and 3 strands of C, ch 65.

Next row: 1 dc in 4th ch from hook. 1 dc in each ch to end of ch. Turn.

Next row: Ch 3. Miss first dc. 1 dc in next dc and each dc to end of row. Turn.

Fold Strap in half lengthwise. Join strap by working 1 sc through tops of corresponding dc and foundation ch to end of row. Fasten off.

Sew on handles as illustrated.

Sarong

SIZES

Approx 40 ins [102 cm] wide x 28 ins [71 cm] long

STITCH GLOSSARY

DcCl: *Yoh and insert hook in next ch or st. Yoh and draw up a loop. Yoh and draw through 2 loops on hook.* Miss next ch or st. Rep from * to * in next ch or st. Yoh and draw through all 3 loops on hook.

MATERIALS

Patons Grace (50 g/1.75 oz)

Main Color (MC) (60104 Azure)	8	**balls**
Contrast A (60005 Snow)	1	**ball**
Contrast B (60409 Ruby)	1	**ball**

Size 4.50 mm (U.S. 7) crochet hook **or size needed to obtain tension**.

TENSION

17 dc and 8 rows = 4 ins [10 cm]

INSTRUCTIONS

With MC, ch 150 (lower edge).

1st row: (RS). 1 dc in 4th ch from hook. Work 1 DcCl inserting hook first in next ch. Ch 1. *Work 1 DcCl inserting hook first in same ch as previous DcCl. Ch 1. Rep from * to end of ch. 1 dc in same ch as last DcCl. Turn.

2nd row: Ch 3 (counts as 1 dc). Miss first st. 1 DcCl inserting hook first in next st. Ch 1. *1 DcCl inserting hook first in same st as previous DcCl. Ch 1. Rep from * to end of row. 1 dc in same st as last DcCl. Turn.

3rd row: Ch 3. 2 dc in first st (double inc made). 1 DcCl inserting hook first in next st. Ch 1. *1 DcCl inserting hook first in same st as previous DcCl. Ch 1. Rep from * to end of row. 3 dc in same st as last DcCl (double inc made).

4th row: Ch 3 (counts as 1 dc). Miss first st. 1 DcCl inserting hook first in next st. Ch 1. *1 DcCl inserting hook first in same st as previous DcCl. Ch 1. Rep from * to end of row. 1 dc in same st as last DcCl. Turn.

Rep last 2 rows 15 times more, taking inc sts into pat.

Cont even in pat until work from beg measures 26 ins [66 cm].

Next row: Ch 1. 1 sc in each st to end of row. Fasten off (top edge).

Edging: Place markers on both sides, 21 rows down from top edge (see diagram). With RS of work facing, join B with sl st at first marker.

1st row: Ch 1. 1 sc in same sp as sl st. Work 2 sc in each post of dc to corner st. 3 sc in corner st. 1 sc in each ch along opposite side of foundation ch to next corner. 3 sc in corner st. Work 2 sc in each post of dc to 2nd marker.

2nd row: Ch 3. Miss first sc. *1 dc in next sc. Ch 1. Miss next sc. Rep from * to end of row. Turn.

3rd row: Ch 2. Miss first dc. *1 hdc in next ch-1 sp. 1 hdc in next dc. Rep from * to end of row, working 3 hdc in corner sts. Join A. Turn.

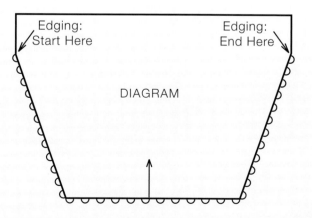

DIAGRAM

4th row: With A, ch 1. 1 sc in first st. *(1 sc. Ch 5. 1 sc) in next st. 1 sc in each of next 7 sts. Rep from * to last 2 sts. (1 sc. Ch 5. 1 sc) in next st. 1 sc in last st. Turn.

5th row: Ch 1. Miss first st. *(1 hdc. 11 dc. 1 hdc) in next ch-5 sp. Miss next st. 1 sc in each of next 5 sts. Rep from * to last ch-5 sp. (1 hdc. 11 dc. 1 hdc) in last ch-5 sp. 1 sc in last st. Join MC. Turn.

6th row: *With MC, ch 4. Miss next hdc and 3 dc. 1 sc in next st. *Ch 3. Sl st in 3rd ch from hook - picot made.* Ch 1. Miss next st. 1 sc in next st. Picot. Ch 1. Miss next st. Picot. Ch 4. Miss next 5 sts. 1 sc in next st. Rep from * to end of row. Fasten off.

Halter Top

SIZE

One Size

MATERIALS

Patons Grace (50 g/1.75 oz)

Main Color (MC) (60027 Ginger)	3	**balls**
Contrast A (60005 Snow)	1	**ball**
Contrast B (60409 Ruby)	1	**ball**

Sizes 2.75 mm (U.S. C or 2) and 3.50 mm (U.S. E or 4) crochet hooks **or size needed to obtain tension**.

TENSION

22 hdc and 15 rows = 4 ins [10 cm] with smaller hook.

INSTRUCTIONS

With smaller hook and MC, ch 111.

1st row: (RS). 1 hdc in 3rd ch from hook. 1 hdc in each ch to end of ch. 110 hdc. Turn.

2nd row: Ch 2 (counts as 1 hdc). Miss first hdc. 1 hdc in each hdc to end of row. 1 hdc in top of ch 2. Turn.

3rd row: Ch 3 (counts as 1 dc). *Yoh and insert hook in next st. Yoh and draw up a loop. Yoh and draw through 2 loops on hook. Miss next st. Yoh and insert hook in next st. Yoh and draw up a loop. Yoh and draw through 2 loops on hook. Yoh and draw through all 3 loops on hook - DcCl made. Ch 1. *Work 1 DcCl inserting hook first in same st as previous DcCl. Ch 1. Rep from * to end of row. 1 dc in same st as last DcCl. Turn.

4th to 6th rows: As 3rd row.

7th row: Ch 2. Miss first st. 1 hdc in each st or ch-1 sp to end of row. 1 hdc in top of ch 3. Turn.

8th row: As 7th row.

9th to 12th rows: As 3rd row.

Rep 7th row until work from beg measures 7 ins [18 cm], ending with RS facing for next row and omitting turning ch at end of last row.

Shape Front: 1st row: 1 sl st in each of first 19 sts. Ch 2. Miss st where last sl st was worked. 1 hdc in each of next 73 hdc. **Turn.** Leave rem 18 sts unworked.

2nd row: Ch 2. Miss first st. *(Yoh and draw up a loop in next st) twice. Yoh and draw through all loops on hook* – hdc2tog made. 1 hdc in each hdc to last 2 sts. Hdc2tog over last 2 sts. Turn. Rep last row 17 times more. 38 sts.

Next row: Ch 2. Miss first st. Hdc2tog over next 2 hdc. 1 hdc in each of next 8 hdc. Hdc2tog over next 2 hdc. **Turn.** Leave rem sts unworked.

**Next row: Ch 2. Miss first st. Hdc2tog over next 2 hdc. 1 hdc in each of next 6 hdc. Hdc2tog over last 2 sts. Turn.

Next row: Ch 2. Miss first st. Hdc2tog over next 2 hdc. 1 hdc in each of next 4 hdc. Hdc2tog over last 2 sts. Turn.

Next row: Ch 2. Miss first st. Hdc2tog over next 2 hdc. 1 hdc in each of next 2 hdc. Hdc2tog over last 2 sts. Turn.

Next row: Ch 2. Miss first st. (Hdc2tog over next 2 sts) twice. Turn.

Next row: Ch 2. Miss first st. Hdc2tog over next 2 sts. Fasten off.**

With RS of work facing, miss next 12 sts. Join MC with sl st to next st.

Next row: Ch 2. Hdc2tog over next 2 hdc. 1 hdc in each of next 8 hdc. Hdc2tog over last 2 sts. Turn. Rep from ** to **.

FINISHING

With RS of work facing and smaller crochet hook, join MC with sl st at 1st row of Front shaping (see diagram). Ch 1. 1 sc in same sp. Work 30 sc along left side to neck edge. Ch 70 for neck tie. Sl st in 2nd ch from hook. Sl st in each ch to end of ch. Work 1 row of sc evenly around neck edge. Ch 70 for neck tie. Sl st in 2nd ch from hook. Sl st in each ch to end of ch. Work 30 sc down right side to 1st row of Front shaping. Fasten off.

With RS of work facing, join MC with sl st at corner of Back opening. Work 40 sc evenly down side of Back opening.

Rep for other side.

Bottom Edging: 1st row: With smaller hook, join B with sl st to first ch of foundation ch. Ch 1. Work 1 sc in each st to last ch. 2 sc in last ch. 111 sc. Turn.

2nd row: Ch 3. Miss first sc. *1 dc in next sc. Ch 1. Miss next sc. Rep from * to last 2 sc. 1 dc in each of last 2 sc. Turn.

3rd row: Ch 2. Miss first dc. *1 hdc in next ch-1 sp. 1 hdc in next dc. Rep from * to end of row. Join A. Turn.

4th row: With A, ch 1. 1 sc in each of first 3 hdc. *(1 sc. Ch 5. 1 sc) in next hdc. 1 sc in each of next 7 hdc. Rep from * to last 4 hdc. (1 sc. Ch 5. 1 sc) in next hdc. 1 sc in each of last 3 hdc. Turn.

5th row: Ch 1. Miss first st. *(1 hdc. 11 dc. 1 hdc) in next ch-5 sp. Miss next st. 1 sc in each of next 5 sts. Rep from * to last ch-5 sp. (1 hdc. 11 dc. 1 hdc) in last ch-5 sp. 1 sc in last st. Join MC. Turn.

6th row: *With MC, ch 4. Miss next hdc and 3 dc. 1 sc in next st. *Ch 3. Sl st in 3rd ch from hook* - picot made. Ch 1. Miss next st. 1 sc in next st. Picot. Ch 1. Miss next st. Picot. Ch 4. Miss next 5 sts. 1 sc in next st. Rep from * to end of row. Fasten off.

Cord: With larger hook and 2 strands of MC, ch 270. Fasten off.

Thread cord through Back as illustrated.

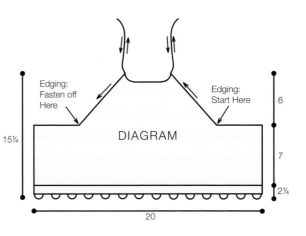

Flirty Floral Halter

SIZES

To fit bust measurement

Extra-Small	32	ins	[81.5		cm]
Small	34	"	[86.5		"]
Medium/Large	36-38	"	[91.5-96.5		"]

MATERIALS

Sizes	XS	S	M/L

Patons Grace (50 g/1.75 oz)

Main Color (MC) (60437 Rose)	4	5	5 **balls**

Small quantities of Contrast A (60604 Terracotta), Contrast B (60603 Apricot) and Contrast C (60409 Ruby)

Sizes 3.00 mm (U.S. C or 2) and 3.50 mm (U.S. E or 4) crochet hooks **or size needed to obtain tension.**

TENSION

$3\frac{1}{2}$ shells and 11 rows = 4 ins [10 cm] in pat with larger hook.

INSTRUCTIONS

The instructions are written for smallest size. If changes are necessary for larger sizes the instructions will be written thus ( ).

FRONT

With larger hook, ch 80 (86**-92).

Foundation row: (RS). 1 sc in 2nd ch from hook. *Miss next 2 ch. *5 dc in next ch* – Shell made. Miss next 2 ch. 1 sc in next ch. Rep from * to end of ch. Turn. 13 (**14**-15) Shells.

1st row: Ch 3. 2 dc in first sc. *Miss next 2 dc. 1 sc in next dc. Miss next 2 dc. Shell in next sc. Rep from * ending with 3 dc in last sc. Turn.

2nd row: Ch 1. 1 sc in first dc. *Miss next 2 dc. Shell in next sc. Miss next 2 dc. 1 sc in next dc. Rep from * ending with 1 sc in top of turning ch. Turn. Last 2 rows form pat.

Cont in pat until work from beg measures 9½ (9½-10½) ins [24 (**24**-27) cm], ending with RS facing for next row.**

Shape top: 1st row: (RS). Sl st in each of first 3 dc. Sl st in next sc. Sl st in each of next 3 dc. Ch 1. 1 sc in same dc as last sl st. Pat to last 9 sts. Miss next 2 dc. 1 sc in next dc. **Turn.** Leave rem sts unworked.

2nd row: Sl st in first sc. Sl st in each of next 3 dc. Ch 1. 1 sc in same dc as last sl st. Pat to last shell. Miss next 2 dc. 1 sc in next dc. **Turn.** Leave rem sts unworked.

Rep last row 4 (**4**-5) times more. 6 (**7**-7) Shells.

Next row: Ch 3. 2 dc in first sc. *Miss next 2 dc. 1 sc in next dc. Miss next 2 dc. Shell in next sc. Rep from * ending with 3 dc in last sc. Turn.

Next row: Ch 1. 1 sc in first dc. *Miss next 2 dc. Shell in next sc. Miss next 2 dc. 1 sc in next dc. Rep from * ending with 1 sc in top of turning ch. Turn. Rep last 2 rows 4 times more. Fasten off.

BACK

Work from ** to ** as given for Front. Fasten off.

Edging: Sew side seams. With RS of work facing and smaller hook, join yarn with sl st to top right corner of Front. Work 1 row of sc evenly down right front shaping, across Back and up left front shaping. **Do not turn.**

Next row: Working from **left** to right instead of from **right** to left as usual, work 1 reverse sc in each sc to end of row. Fasten off.

Casing: Fold last 2 rows of Front to WS and sew in position leaving ends open to insert neck tie.

INSTRUCTIONS CONT.

Neck Tie: With larger hook, make a chain 48 ins [122 cm] long. Turn chain sideways. Sl st in center 'bump' at back of 2nd ch from hook. Sl st in next bump and each bump to end of ch. Fasten off.

Flowers [Make 10 (**11**-12) each with A, B and C] With smaller hook, ch 5. Join with sl st to first ch to form ring.

1st rnd: (Ch 3. 1 dc in ring. Ch 3. Sl st in ring) 6 times. Fasten off leaving an end approx 6 ins [15 cm] long to sew Flower to garment. Sew Flowers around bottom edge of garment altering colors as illustrated.

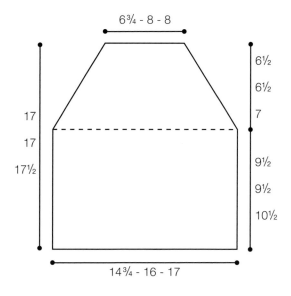

Kaleidoscope Shawl

MEASUREMENT

Approx 60 ins [152.5 cm] wide x 25 ins [63.5 cm] deep (excluding tassels).

MATERIALS

Patons Grace (50 g/1.75 oz)

Main Color (MC) (60437 Rose)	7	**balls**
Contrast A (60604 Terracotta)	5	**balls**
Contrast B (60603 Apricot)	4	**balls**
Contrast C (60409 Ruby)	2	**balls**

Sizes 3.50 mm (U.S. D or 3) crochet hook **or size needed to obtain tension**.

TENSION

One Motif = Approx 5 ins [12.5 cm] long on each side.

INSTRUCTIONS

With C, ch 5. Join with sl st to first ch to form ring.

1st rnd: Ch 3. (Yoh and draw up a loop in ring. Yoh and draw through 2 loops on hook) twice. Yoh and draw through all loops on hook – Dc2tog made. Ch 5. *(Yoh and draw up a loop in ring. Yoh and draw through 2 loops on hook) 3 times. Yoh and draw through all loops on hook –* Dc3tog made. *Ch 3. Dc3tog. Ch 5. Dc3tog. Rep from * once more. Ch 3. Join B with sl st to top of ch 3.

2nd rnd: With B, sl st in next ch 5 sp. Ch 3. Dc2tog in same sp. Ch 4. [(Yoh) twice and draw up a loop in same ch-5 sp. (Yoh and draw through 2 loops on hook) twice] 3 times. Yoh and draw through all loops on hook - Tr3tog made. Ch 5. Sl st in top of Tr3tog – Picot made. Ch 4. Dc3tog in same ch-5 sp. *Ch 3. 1 sc in next ch-3 sp. Ch 3. (Dc3tog. Ch 4. Tr3tog. Picot. Ch 4. Dc3tog) all in next ch-5 sp. Rep from * once more. Ch 3. 1 sc in next ch-3 sp. Ch 3. Join A with sl st to top of ch 3.

3rd rnd: With A, ch 3. 5 dc in next ch-4 sp. *(2 dc. Ch 5. 2 dc) in next Picot. 5 dc in next ch-4 sp. 3 dc in next ch-3 sp. 1 dc in next sc.** 3 dc in next ch-3 sp. 5 dc in next ch-4 sp. Rep from * once more, then from * to ** once. 2 dc in last ch 3 sp. Join MC with sl st to top of ch 3.

4th rnd: With MC, sl st in next dc. Ch 4 (counts as dc and ch 1). (Miss next dc. 1 dc in next dc. Ch 1) 3 times. *(Dc3tog. Ch 3. Tr3tog. Picot. Ch 3. Dc3tog) in next ch-5 sp. Ch 1.** (1 dc in next dc. Ch 1. Miss next dc) 10 times. 1 dc in next dc. Ch 1. Rep from * once more, then from * to ** once. (1 dc in next dc. Ch 1. Miss next dc) 7 times. Ch 1. Join with sl st to 3rd ch of ch 4. Fasten off.

Joining Motifs: Follow diagram for Motif placement, working joining sides on 4th rnd as follows: *(Dc3tog. Ch 3. Tr3tog. Ch 2. Sl st in corresponding corner of joining Motif. Ch 2. Sl st in Tr3tog. Ch 3. Dc3tog) in next ch-5 sp.* Ch 1. Sl st in corresponding ch-1 sp of joining Motif. Ch 1. (1 dc in next dc. Ch 1. Sl st in corresponding ch-1 sp of joining Motif. Ch 1. Miss next dc) 10 times. 1 dc in next dc. Ch 1. Sl st in corresponding ch-1 sp of joining Motif. Ch 1. Rep from * to * for next corner. Rep this side as appropriate to join Motifs. Complete 4th rnd as for Motif 1. (70 Motifs in total).

TASSELS: (Make 8).

Cut a piece of cardboard 4.5 ins [11 cm] wide. Wind MC around cardboard 25 times. Break yarn leaving a long end and thread end through a needle. Slip needle through all loops and tie tightly. Remove cardboard and wind yarn tightly around loops ¾ inch [2 cm] below fold. Fasten securely. Cut through rem loops and trim ends evenly. Sew one tassel to each point of Shawl as shown in picture.

DIAGRAM

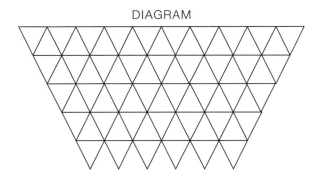

Accessories

Appliqué Kerchief & Scarf

SIZES

Kerchief: One size to fit Average Youth/Lady

Scarf: Approx 8 ins [20.5 cm] wide x 62 ins [157.5 cm] long

MATERIALS

Patons Classic Wool (100 g/3.5 oz)

Kerchief and Scarf

Main Color (MC) (205 Deep Olive)	3	balls
Contrast A (206 Russet)	1	ball
Contrast B (240 Leaf Green)	1	ball

Sizes 4.50 mm (U.S. 7) and 5.00 mm (U.S. H or 8) crochet hooks **or size needed to obtain tension.**

TENSION

5½ shells and 8 rows = 4 ins [10 cm] with larger hook in pat.

INSTRUCTIONS

Kerchief

With MC and larger hook, ch 5.

Foundation row: 1 dc in 5th ch from hook. Ch 4. Turn.

1st row: 1 dc in first dc. *(1 dc. Ch 1. 1 dc) all in 3rd ch of turning ch* – shell made. Ch 4. Turn.

2nd row: 1 dc in first dc. Shell in next sp between 2 shells. Shell in 3rd ch of turning ch. Ch 4. Turn.

3rd row: 1 dc in first dc. *Shell in next sp between 2 shells. Rep from * to last shell. Shell in 3rd ch of turning ch. Ch 4. Turn.

Rep last row until there are 26 shells in row ending last row with ch 37. Turn.

Next row: Sl st in 2nd ch from hook. 1 sl st in each of next 35 ch. 1 sc in each dc or ch-1 sp across, ending with 1 sc in ch-4 sp. 1 sc in 3rd ch of turning ch. Ch 37. Turn.

Next row: Sl st in 2nd ch from hook. 1 sl st in each of next 35 ch. Sl st in next sc. Fasten off.

FLOWER APPLIQUÉ

With B and smaller hook, ch 4.

1st rnd: Work 11 dc in 4th ch from hook. Join A with sl st to top of ch 3. 12 dc in rnd.

2nd rnd: With A, ch 4. *[(Yoh) twice and draw up a loop. (Yoh and draw through 2 loops on hook) twice] twice in next dc. Yoh and draw through all loops on hook – tr2tog made. Ch 4. Sl st in next dc. Ch 4. Rep from * around to last dc. Tr2tog in last dc. Ch 4. Join with sl st in same sp as first ch 4. Fasten off.

Sew Flower Appliqué to Kerchief as illustrated.

Scarf

Pocket (make 2)

With MC and larger hook, ch 17.

Foundation row: 1 dc in 5th ch from hook. (Miss next 2 ch. Shell in next ch) 4 times. Ch 4. Turn.

1st row: 1 dc in first dc. (Shell in next sp between 2 shells) 4 times. Shell in 3rd ch of turning ch. Ch 4. Turn.

2nd row: 1 dc in first dc. (Shell in next sp between 2 shells) 5 times. Shell in 3rd ch of turning ch. Ch 4. Turn.

3rd row: 1 dc in first dc. (Shell in next sp between 2 shells) 6 times. Shell in 3rd ch of turning ch. Ch 4. Turn.

4th row: (Shell in next sp between 2 shells) 7 times. Shell in 3rd ch of turning ch. Ch 1. 1 dc in 3rd ch of turning ch. Ch 4. Turn.

Rep last row 7 times more, omitting turning ch at end of last row. Fasten off.

Scarf: With MC and larger hook, ch 34.

Foundation row: Shell in 5th ch from hook. (Miss next 2 ch. Shell in next ch) 9 times. Miss next ch. 1 dc in last ch. Ch 4. Turn.

1st row: 1 dc in first dc. (Shell in next sp between 2 shells) 9 times. Shell in top of turning ch. Ch 3. Turn.

2nd row: (Shell in next sp between 2 shells) 10 times. 1 dc in 3rd ch of turning ch. Ch 4. Turn.

Rep last 2 rows until Scarf from beg measures 62 ins [157.5 cm] omitting turning ch at end of last row. Fasten off.

Flower Appliqué: Make 2 as given for Kerchief. Sew Flower Appliqué to each Pocket as illustrated. Sew Pockets in position.

On the Wild Side Set

MEASUREMENTS

Scarf: Measures approx 8½ x 60 ins [21.5 x 152 cm] (excluding fringe).

Hat: One size to fit average lady.

Bag: Measures approx 10 x 12 ins [25.5 x 30.5 cm] excluding fridge and handle.

MATERIALS

Patons Shetland Chunky (100 g/3.5 oz)

	Scarf	Hat	Bag	
Main Color (MC) (03031) Earthy Brown				
	1	1	1	**ball**
Contrast A (03108 Med Blue or 03315 Amethyst)				
	1	1	1	**ball**
Contrast B (03020 Deep Taupe)				
	1	1	1	**ball**
Contrast C (03430 Wine)				
	1	1	1	**ball**

Sizes 6.50 mm (U.S. K or 10½) and 9 mm (U.S. M or 13) crochet hooks or size needed to obtain tension. 2 metal macrame rings 6 ins [15 cm] diameter for bag.

TENSION

Large Motif = 3½ ins [9 cm]
12 dc and 6 rows = 4 ins [10 cm] with smaller crochet hook.

INSTRUCTIONS

Note: *Ch 2 does not counts as hdc.*

Scarf

FIRST LARGE MOTIF

With smaller hook and A, ch 4. Join in a ring.

1st rnd: Ch 1. 12 sc in ring. Join B with sl st to first sc.

2nd rnd: With B, ch 3 (counts as dc). 1 dc in same sp as sl st. 1 dc in next sc. *2 dc in next sc. 1 dc in next sc. Rep from * to end of rnd. Join C with sl st to top of ch 3. 18 dc.

3rd rnd: With C, ch 2. 2 hdc in same sp as sl st. *2 hdc in each dc around. Join with sl st to first hdc. Fasten off. 36 hdc.

SECOND LARGE MOTIF (joining 2 Large motifs)

Work 1st and 2nd rnds as given for First Large Motif.

3rd rnd: With C, ch 2. 2 hdc in same sp as sl st. 2 hdc in each of next 8 dc. Join with sl st to any hdc of First Large Motif – Joint I made. 2 hdc in each dc to end of rnd. Join with sl st to first hdc. Fasten off. 36 hdc.

First set of 2 Large Motifs complete.

Make 11 more sets.

**MEDIUM MOTIF (joining to 4 Large Motifs)

(See diagram on page 51.)

With MC, ch 4. Join in a ring.

1st rnd: Ch 4 (counts as dc and ch 1). 1 dc in ring. Ch 1. *Join with sl st in 6th hdc of First Large Motif before Joint I – Joint II made. (1 dc. Ch 1) twice in ring. Miss 5 hdc after Joint I on Second Large Motif. Join with sl st to next hdc of Second Large Motif – Joint III made*. (1 dc. Ch 1) 4 times in ring. Rep from * to * on second set of Large Motifs. (1 dc. Ch 1) 3 times in ring. Join with sl st to 3rd ch of beg ch 4. Fasten off. 12 dc.

FIRST SMALL MOTIF (Joining to 2 Large and Medium Motifs)

With A, ch 4. Join in a ring.

1st rnd: Ch 3 (counts as dc). 2 dc in ring. Join with sl st to 4th hdc before Joint II of second set of Large Motifs - Joint IV made. 3 dc in ring. Miss (dc, ch 1, dc, ch 1) of Medium Motif from Joint II. Join with sl st to next dc of Medium Motif - Joint V made. 3 dc in ring. Miss 3 dc of Large Motif from Joint III. Join with sl st to Large Motif - Joint VI made. 3 dc in ring. Join with sl st to first dc. Fasten off. 12 dc.

Rep for Second Small Motif, joined to opposite side of Medium Motif.**

Rep from ** to ** until all 12 sets of Large Motifs have been joined.

Border: With RS of Scarf facing miss 3 dc of First Large Motif from Small Motif Join, join MC with sl st to 4th hdc of First Large Motif. Working into **back** loops only, ch 3 (counts as dc). **1 hdc in next hdc. (1 sc in next hdc. Ch 1. Miss next hdc) twice. 1 sc in next hdc. 1 hdc in next hdc. 1 dc in next hdc. Ch 2 (corner). 1 dc in next hdc. 1 hdc in next hdc. (1 sc in next hdc. Ch 1. Miss next hdc) twice. 1 sc in next hdc. 1 hdc in next hdc. 1 dc in next hdc. Ch 2.** Miss 4 hdc from Joint I of 2nd Large Motif. 1 dc in 5th hdc of 2nd Large Motif. Rep from ** to ** once more. ***Miss 2 dc from Joint of Small Motif. 1 tr in each of next 3 dc of Small Motif. Ch 2. Miss next 3 hdc of Large Motif from Joint. 1 dc in 4th hdc of Large Motif. 1 hdc in next hdc. (1 sc in next hdc. Ch 1. Miss next st) twice. 1 sc in next hdc. 1 hdc in next hdc. 1 dc in next hdc. Ch 2.*** Rep from *** to *** along side of Scarf to last Large Motif. Miss 3 hdc of Large Motif from Joint. Rep from ** to ** twice around the other end of Scarf. Work from *** to *** along other side of Scarf, ending with sl st to top of beg ch 3. Fasten off.

Fringe: Cut length of A, B and C, 15 ins [38 cm] long. Taking 3 strands each of A, B and C tog, knot into fringe across ends of Scarf. Trim fringe evenly.

DIAGRAM

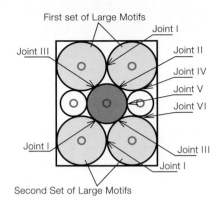

First set of Large Motifs

Joint III   Joint I   Joint II

Joint IV

Joint V

Joint VI

Joint I   Joint III

Joint I

Second Set of Large Motifs

Hat

MOTIF I

**With smaller hook and A, ch 4. Join in a ring.

1st rnd: Ch 1. 12 sc in ring. Fasten off.

2nd rnd: Join B with sl st to any sc. Ch 3 (counts as dc). 1 dc in same sp as sl st. 2 dc in next sc. 1 dc in next sc. *(2 dc in next sc) twice. 1 dc in next sc. Rep from * around. Join with sl st to top of ch 3. 20 dc. Fasten off.**

3rd rnd: Join C with sl st to any dc. Ch 2. 1 hdc in each of first 3 dc. 1 dc in next dc. Ch 3. (1 dc in next dc. 1 hdc in each of next 3 dc. 1 dc in next dc. Ch 3) 3 times. 1 dc in next dc. Join with sl st to first hdc. Fasten off.

INSTRUCTIONS CONT.

MOTIFS II TO V

Work from ** to ** as given for Motif I.

3rd rnd: Join C with sl st to any dc. Ch 2. 1 hdc in each of first 3 dc. 1 dc in next dc. (Ch 3. 1 dc in next dc. 1 hdc in each of next 3 dc. 1 dc in next dc) twice. Ch 1. Join with sl st to corner of previous motif. Ch 1. 1 dc in next dc. 1 hdc in next dc. Miss next dc and hdc of previous motif. Join with sl st to 2nd hdc of joining motif. 1 hdc in each of next 2 dc. 1 dc in next dc. Ch 1. 1 dc in next dc. Miss next hdc and dc of joining motif. Join with sl st to corner of previous motif. Ch 1. 1 dc in next dc. Join with sl st to first hdc. Fasten off.

MOTIF VI

Work from ** to ** as given for Motif I.

3rd rnd: Join C with sl st to any dc. Ch 2 (counts as hdc). 1 hdc in each of next 2 dc. 1 dc in next dc. *Ch 1. Join with sl st to corner of previous motif. Ch 1. 1 dc in next dc. 1 hdc in next dc. Miss next dc and hdc in previous motif. Join with sl st to 2nd hdc of previous motif. 1 hdc in each of next 2 dc. 1 dc in next dc. Ch 1. Miss next hdc and dc of previous motif. Join with sl st to corner of previous motif.* Ch 1. 1 dc in next dc. 1 hdc in each of next 3 dc. 1 dc in next dc.

Rep from * to *, joining to Motif I instead of previous motif. Join with sl st to first hdc. Fasten off.

These 6 motifs form crown of hat.

TOP OF HAT

Note: To change color, work to last 2 loops on hook of first color. Draw loop in next color through 2 loops on hook to complete st and proceed in next color.

1st rnd: (RS). Join MC with sl st to sp between motifs. Ch 2. 1 hdc in same sp as last sl st. Work 8 hdc across first motif. *1 hdc in sp between motifs. 8 hdc across next motif. Rep from * around. Join with sl st to first hdc. 54 hdc.

2nd rnd: Ch 2. 1 hdc in each hdc around. Join A with sl st to first hdc. Break MC.

3rd rnd: With A, ch 2. 1 hdc in each of first 8 hdc. Miss next hdc. *1 hdc in each of next 8 hdc. Miss next hdc. Rep from * around. Join B with sl st to first hdc. 48 hdc. Break A.

4th rnd: With B, ch 2. 1 hdc in each of first 7 hdc. Miss next hdc. *1 hdc in each of next 7 hdc. Miss next hdc. Rep from * around. Join C with sl st to first hdc. 42 hdc. Break B.

5th rnd: With C, ch 2. 1 hdc in each of first 6 hdc. Miss next hdc. *1 hdc in each of next 6 hdc. Miss next hdc. Rep from * around. Join MC with sl st to first hdc. 36 hdc. Break C.

6th rnd: With MC, ch 2. 1 hdc in each of first 5 hdc. Miss next hdc. *1 hdc in each of next 5 hdc. Miss next hdc. Rep from * around. Join A with sl st to first hdc. 30 hdc. Break MC.

7th rnd: With A, ch 2. 1 hdc in each of first 2 hdc. Miss next hdc. *1 hdc in each of next 2 hdc. Miss next hdc. Rep from * around. Join with sl st to first hdc. 20 hdc.

8th rnd: Ch 2. Yoh and draw up a loop in each of first 4 hdc. Yoh and draw through all 4 loops on hook. (draw up a loop in each of next 4 hdc. Yoh and draw through all 5 loops on hook) 4 times. Fasten off.

Edging: 1st rnd: Join MC with sl st between any 2 motifs at lower edge. Ch 1. Work 1 sc in same sp as last sl st. *Work 8 sc across motif and 1 sc in sp between motifs. Rep from * around Hat. Join with sl st to first sc.

2nd rnd: Ch 1. Work 1 sc in each sc around. Join with sl st to first sc. Fasten off.

Bag (make 2 pieces alike)

STRIPE PATTERN

Work 1 row with MC.

Work 1 row with A.

Work 1 row with B.

Work 1 row with C.

These 4 rows form Stripe Pat.

With smaller hook and MC, ch 31.

Foundation row: (RS). 1 dc in 4th ch from hook. 1 dc in each of next 2 ch. *Ch 1. Miss next ch. 1 dc in each of next 4 ch. Rep from * to end of ch. Join A in last dc. Ch 3. Turn. 30 sts.

1st row: With A, miss first dc. 1 dc in each of next 3 dc. *Ch 1. Miss next ch-1 sp. 1 dc in each of next 4 dc. Rep from * to end of row. Join B in last dc. Ch 3. Turn.

Last row forms pat.

2nd row of Stripe Pat is complete.

Keeping cont of Stripe Pat (beg with 3rd row), work a further 10 rows in pat, ending with RS facing for next row. Place markers at each end of last row.

Shape top: 13th row: With MC, miss first dc. *(Yoh and draw up a loop in next dc. Yoh and draw through 2 loops on hook) twice. Yoh and draw through all 3 loops on hook – dc2tog made.* Pat to last 3 sts. Dc2tog over next 2 sts. 1 dc in last dc. Join A, ch 3. Turn.

14th row: With A, miss first dc. Dc2tog over next 2 dc. Pat to last 3 dc. Dc2tog over next 2 dc. 1 dc in last dc. Join B, ch 3. Turn.

15th row: Miss first dc. 1 dc in next dc. Ch 1. Miss next ch-1 sp. Dc2tog over next 2 dc. Pat to last 5 sts. Dc2tog over next 2 dc. Ch 1. Miss next ch-1 sp. 1 dc in each of last 2 dc. Join C, ch 3. Turn.

INSTRUCTIONS CONT.

16th row: Miss first dc. 1 dc in next dc. Ch 1. Miss next ch-1 sp. Dc2tog over next 2 dc. Pat to last 5 sts. Dc2tog over next 2 dc. Ch 1. Miss next ch-1 sp. 1 dc in each of last 2 dc. Join MC, ch 3. Turn.

17th row: Miss first dc. 1 dc in next dc. Ch 1. Miss next ch-1 sp. Dc2tog over next 2 dc. Pat to last 5 sts. Dc2tog over next 2 dc. Ch 1. Miss next ch-1 sp. 1 dc in each of last 2 dc. Join A, ch 3. Turn.

18th, 19th, 20th and 21st rows: Miss first dc. 1 dc in next dc. Ch 1. Miss next ch-1 sp. 1 dc in next dc. Pat to last 4 sts. 1 dc in next dc. Ch 1. Miss next ch-1 sp. 1 dc in each of last 2 dc. Ch 3. Turn. Omit turning ch at end of last row. Fasten off.

Handles: With larger hook and 3 strands of MC, work 1 rnd of sc around each ring. Join with sl st to first sc. Fasten off.

Fold last 2 rows of Bag to inside and sew over Handles to form casing. With MC, sew Bag tog, beg and ending at markers.

Fringe: Cut lengths of A, B and C, 9 ins [23 cm] long. Taking 2 strands each of A, B and C tog, knot into fringe across lower edge of Bag in each corner, then at every point where ch-1 sp occurs in pat. Trim fringe evenly.

Allure I-Piece Poncho

SIZES

To fit bust measurement

Extra-Small/Medium
   28-38 ins   [71-96.5   cm]

Large/2-XLarge
   40-50 "   [101.5-127 "]

3 XLarge/5-XLarge
   52-62 "   [132-157.5 "]

Finished length between neck edge and point

X-S/M	17 ins	[43 cm]
L/2-XL	19¾ "	[50 "]
3-XL/5-XL	22½ "	[57 "]

STITCH GLOSSARY

beg = Beginning.

Ch = Chain.

Rep = Repeat.

RS = Right side.

sc = Single crochet.

sp(s) = Space(s).

MATERIALS

Patons Allure (50 g/1.75 oz)

04405 (Ruby)

Sizes	XS/M	L/2XL	3XL/5XL	
	8	9	10	balls

Size 8 mm (U.S. 11) crochet hook **or size needed to obtain tension**.

Optional: 50 ins [127 cm] length of ½ inch [1.5 cm] wide ribbon for Drawstring.

TENSION

9 sts and 9 rows = 4 ins [10 cm] in pattern.

INSTRUCTIONS

Ch 29 (**31**-37).

Foundation row: (RS). 1 sc in 2nd ch from hook. 1 sc in each ch to end of ch. Turn. 28 (**30**-36) sc.

1st row: Ch 1. 1 sc in first sc. *Ch 1. Miss next sc. 1 sc in next sc. Rep from * to last sc. 1 sc in last sc. Turn.

2nd row: Ch 1. 1 sc in first sc. *Ch 1. Miss next sc. 1 sc in next ch-1 sp. Rep from * to last sc. 1 sc in last sc. Turn.

Rep last row until work from beg measures 51 (**53**-55) ins [129.5 (**134.5**-139.5) cm], ending with RS facing for next row.

Next row: Ch 1. 1 sc in each of first 2 sc. *1 sc in next ch-1 sp. 1 sc in next sc. Rep from * to end of row. Fasten off.

FINISHING

Sew as illustrated in Diagram.

Yarn Drawstring: Make a chain 50 ins [127 cm] long. Fasten off.

Starting at center front, thread drawstring through ch-1 sps along neck edge as shown in picture.

Optional: Ribbon Drawstring: Starting at center front, thread ribbon along neck edge.

Optional: Embellish Poncho with brooch(es) as shown on picture.

DIAGRAM

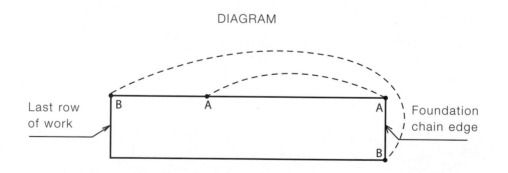

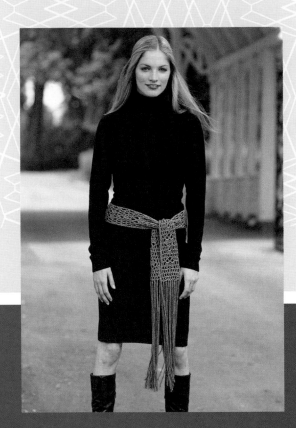

Light & Lacy Scarf and Belt

MEASUREMENTS

Scarf: Approx 3 x 72 ins [7.5 x 182.5 cm] (excluding fringe).

Belt: Approx 4 x 44 ins [10 x 112 cm] (excluding fringe).

MATERIALS

Patons Katrina (100 g)

Scarf
Dusk (10425)   2   **balls**

Belt
Iris (10315)   2   **balls**

Size 5.50 mm (U.S. I or 9) crochet hook or size needed to obtain tension.

TENSION

17 sts and 7 rows = 4 ins [10 cm] in pattern.

INSTRUCTIONS

Scarf

Ch 16.

1st row: (RS). 1 dc in 6th ch from hook (counts as 1 dc. Ch 1. 1 dc). *Ch 1. Miss next ch. 1 dc in next ch. Rep from * to end of chain. Turn. 7 dc.

2nd row: Ch 3 (counts as dc). (1 dc in next ch-1 sp. Ch 1. Miss next dc) 5 times. 1 dc in last ch-1 sp. 1 dc in 5th ch of ch 6. Turn. 8 dc.

3rd row: Ch 4 (counts as 1 dc. Ch 1). Miss first 2 dc. (1 dc in next ch-1 sp. Ch 1. Miss next dc) 5 times. 1 dc in top of ch 3. Turn. 7 dc.

4th row: Ch 3 (counts as dc). 1 dc in next ch-1 sp. Ch 1. Miss next dc. 1 dc in next ch-1 sp. Miss next dc and ch-1 sp. (1 dc. Ch 2. 1 dc) all in next dc. Miss next ch-1 sp and dc. 1 dc in next ch-1 sp. Ch 1. Miss next dc. 1 dc in next ch-1 sp. 1 dc in 3rd ch of ch 4. Turn.

5th row: Ch 4 (counts as 1 dc. Ch 1). Miss first 2 dc. 1 dc in next ch-1 sp. Ch 1. Miss next 2 dc. (2 dc. Ch 2. 2 dc) all in next ch-2 sp. Ch 1. Miss next 2 dc. 1 dc in next ch-1 sp. Ch 1. Miss next dc. 1 dc in top of ch 3. Turn.

6th row: Ch 3 (counts as dc). 1 dc in next ch-1 sp. Ch 1. 1 dc in next ch-1 sp. Miss next 2 dc. Ch 2. 1 sc in next ch-2 sp. Ch 2. Miss next 2 dc. 1 dc in next ch-1 sp. Ch 1. Miss next dc. 1 dc in next ch-1 sp. 1 dc in 3rd ch of ch 4. Turn.

7th row: Ch 4 (counts as 1 dc. Ch 1). Miss first 2 dc. 1 dc in next ch-1 sp. Ch 1. 1 dc in next ch-2 sp. Ch 1. 1 dc in next sc. Ch 1. 1 dc in next ch-2 sp. Ch 1. Miss next dc. 1 dc in next ch-1 sp. Ch 1. Miss next dc. 1 dc in top of ch 3. Turn.

8th row: Ch 3 (counts as dc). (1 dc in next ch-1 sp. Ch 1. Miss next dc) 5 times. 1 dc in last ch-1 sp. 1 dc in 3rd ch of ch 4. Turn. 8 dc.

Rep 3rd to 8th rows for Pat.

Work a further 121 rows in pat, ending on a 3rd row of Pat. Fasten off.

Fringe: Take 2 strands of yarn 40 ins [101.5 cm] long, fold in half and knot into fringe to each end of Scarf. Trim fringe evenly.

Belt

Ch 20.

1st row: (RS). 1 dc in 6th ch from hook (counts as 1 dc. Ch 1. 1 dc). *Ch 1. Miss next ch. 1 dc in next ch. Rep from * to end of row. Turn. 9 dc.

2nd row: Ch 3 (counts as dc). (1 dc in next ch-1 sp. Ch 1. Miss next dc) 7 times. 1 dc in last ch-1 sp. 1 dc in 5th ch of ch 6. Turn. 10 dc.

3rd row: Ch 4 (counts as 1 dc. Ch 1). Miss first 2 dc. (1 dc in next ch-1 sp. Ch 1. Miss next dc) 7 times. 1 dc in top of ch 3. Turn. 9 dc.

4th row: Ch 3 (counts as dc). 1 dc in next ch-1 sp. Ch 1. Miss next dc. 1 dc in next ch-1 sp. Miss next dc and ch 1. (1 dc. Ch 2. 1 dc) all in next dc. Miss next (Ch 1. 1 dc. Ch 1). (1 dc. Ch 2. 1 dc) all in next dc. Miss next (Ch 1. 1 dc). 1 dc in next ch-1 sp. Ch 1. Miss next dc. 1 dc in last ch-1 sp. 1 dc in 3rd ch of ch 4. Turn.

5th row: Ch 4 (counts as 1 dc. Ch 1). Miss first 2 dc. 1 dc in next ch-1 sp. *Ch 1. Miss next 2 dc. (2 dc. Ch 2. 2 dc) all in next ch 2 sp. Rep from * once more. Miss next 2 dc. 1 dc in next ch-1 sp. Ch 1. Miss next dc. 1 dc in top of ch 3. Turn.

6th row: Ch 3 (counts as dc). 1 dc in first ch-1 sp. Ch 1. Miss next dc. *1 dc in next ch-1 sp. Ch 2. Miss next 2 dc. 1 sc in next ch-2 sp. Ch 2. Miss next 2 dc. Rep from * once more. 1 dc in next ch-1 sp. Ch 1. Miss next dc. 1 dc in last ch-1 sp. 1 dc in 3rd ch of ch 4. Turn.

7th row: Ch 4 (counts as 1 dc. Ch 1). Miss first 2 dc. 1 dc in next ch-1 sp. Ch 1. Miss next dc. 1 dc in next ch-2 sp. Ch 1. 1 dc in next sc. Miss next ch-2 sp. (1 dc. Ch 2. 1 dc) all in next dc. Miss next ch-2 sp. 1 dc in next sc. Ch 1. 1 dc in next ch-2 sp. Ch 1. Miss next dc. 1 dc in next ch-1 sp. Ch 1. Miss next dc. 1 dc in top of ch 3. Turn.

8th row: Ch 3 (counts as dc). (1 dc in next ch-1 sp. Ch 1. Miss next dc) twice. 1 dc in next ch-1 sp. Ch 1. Miss next 2 dc. (2 dc. Ch 2. 2 dc) all in next ch 2 sp. Ch 1. Miss next 2 dc. (1 dc in next ch-1 sp. Ch 1. Miss next dc) twice. 1 dc in last ch-1 sp. 1 dc in 3rd ch of ch 4. Turn.

9th row: Ch 4 (counts as 1 dc. Ch 1). Miss first 2 dc. (1 dc in next ch-1 sp. Ch 1. Miss next dc) twice. 1 dc in next ch-1 sp. Ch 2. Miss next 2 dc. 1 sc in next ch-2 sp. Ch 2. (1 dc in next ch 1 sp. Ch 1. Miss next dc) 3 times. 1 dc in top of ch 3. Turn.

10th row: As 4th row.

Rep 5th to 10th row 11 times more, then rep 5th and 6th rows once.

Next row: Ch 4 (counts as 1 dc. Ch 1). Miss first 2 dc. 1 dc in next ch-1 sp. Ch 1. Miss next dc. 1 dc in next ch-2 sp. Ch 1. 1 dc in next sc. Ch 1. Miss next ch 2 sp. 1 dc in next dc. Ch 1. Miss next ch-2 sp. 1 dc in next sc. Ch 1. 1 dc in next ch-2 sp. Ch 1. Miss next dc. 1 dc in next ch-1 sp. Ch 1. Miss next dc. 1 dc in top of ch 3. Turn.

Next row: Ch 3 (counts as dc). (1 dc in next ch-1 sp. Ch 1. Miss next dc) 7 times. 1 dc in last ch-1 sp. 1 dc in 3rd ch of ch 4. Turn.

Next row: Ch 4 (counts as 1 dc. Ch 1). Miss first 2 dc. (1 dc in next ch-1 sp. Ch 1. Miss next dc) 7 times. 1 dc in top of ch 3. Fasten off.

Fringe: Work as given for Scarf. (See diagram on page 54.)

Crochet Canadiana Scarf

MEASUREMENT

Scarf: 6 x 57 ins [15 x 144.5 cm] without fringe.

MATERIALS

Patons Canadiana (100 g)

Main Color (MC) (0005) Cardinal   1 ball
Color A (432) School Bus Yellow   1 ball
Color B (10416) Super Pink   1 ball
Color C (00030) Med Blue   1 ball

Sizes 4.5 mm (U.S.7) crochet hook **or size needed to obtain tension.**

TENSION

9 dc and 8 rows = 4 ins [10 cm] in pattern.

INSTRUCTIONS

With MC, ch 262.

Foundation Row: 1 dc in 3rd ch from hook (counts as 1 dc). 1 dc in next ch. *Ch 1. Miss next ch. 1 dc in next ch. Rep from * to end of ch. Break MC leaving a 7 ins [18cm] long end. 260 sts.

1st row: Join A, leaving a 7 ins [18cm] long end for fringe. Ch 3 (counts as 1 dc). *1 dc in next ch 1 sp. Ch 1. Miss next dc. Rep from * to last dc. 1 dc in top of ch 3 from previous row. Break yarn leaving a 7 ins [18 cm] long end.

2nd row: Join B and work as 1st row.

3rd row: Join C and work as 1st row

4th row: Join MC and work as 1st row.

5th row: Join A and work as 1st row.

6th row: Join MC and work as 1st row.

7th row: Join C and work as 1st row.

8th row: Join B and work as 1st row.

9th row: Join A and work as 1st row.

10th row: Join MC and work as 1st row.

Fringe: Cut 14 ins [35.5 cm] lengths of yarn and taking 3 strands of each corresponding color, knot into fringe across top and bottom of Scarf. Trim fringe evenly.

Cloche Hat and Mittens

SIZES

One size to fit Average Lady

MATERIALS

Patons Shetland Chunky (100 g/3.5 oz)

Mittens (03607 Harvest Variegate)   1   **ball**

Hat (03607 Harvest Variegate)   1   **ball**

Sizes 5.50 mm (U.S. I or 9) and 6.00 mm (U.S. J or 10) crochet hooks **or size needed to obtain tension.**

TENSION

12 sc and 14 rows = 4 ins [10 cm] with larger hook.

INSTRUCTIONS

Mittens

RIGHT MITTEN

**With smaller hook, ch 8.

1st row: 1 sc in 2nd ch from hook. 1 sc in each ch to end of ch. 7 sc. Turn.

2nd row: Ch 1. Working in back loops only, 1 sc in first sc. 1 sc in each sc to end of row.

Rep last row until work, when slightly stretched, measures 7 ins [18 cm].

Change to larger hook. Ch 1. Turn and working along side edge of ribbing, proceed as follows:

1st row: Work 25 sc along side edge evenly spaced. Turn.

2nd row: Ch 1. 1 sc in each sc to end of row.

Rep last row until Mitten above cuff measures 1½ ins [4 cm], ending with RS facing for next row.**

Shape thumb gusset: 1st row: Ch 1. 1 sc in each of next 14 sc. 2 sc in next sc. 1 sc in next sc. 2 sc in next sc. 1 sc in each of next 8 sc. Turn.

2nd row: Ch 1. 1 sc in each of next 8 sc. 2 sc in next sc. 1 sc in each of next 3 sc. 2 sc in next sc. 1 sc in each of next 14 sc. Turn.

3rd row: Ch 1. 1 sc in each of next 14 sc. 2 sc in next sc. 1 sc in each of next 5 sc. 2 sc in next sc. 1 sc in each of next 8 sc. Turn.

4th row: Ch 1. 1 sc in each of next 8 sc. 2 sc in next sc. 1 sc in each of next 7 sc. 2 sc in next sc. 1 sc in each of next 14 sc. Turn.

5th row: Ch 1. 1 sc in each of next 14 sc. 2 sc in next sc. 1 sc in each of next 9 sc. 2 sc in next sc. 1 sc in each of next 8 sc. Turn.

6th row: Ch 1. 1 sc in each of next 9 sc. Ch 1 (place marker for thumb). Miss next 11 sc. 1 sc in each of next 15 sc. 25 sts. Turn.

7th row: Ch 1. 1 sc in each st and ch 1 sp to end of row. Turn.

Cont even until Mitten above cuff measures 6½ ins [16.5 cm], ending with RS facing for next row.

***Proceed as follows:

1st row: Ch 1. *Draw up a loop in each of first 2 sts. Yoh and draw through all loops on hook* – sc2tog made. 1 sc in each of next 8 sc. Sc2tog over next 2 sc. 1 sc in next sc. Sc2tog over next 2 sc. 1 sc in each of next 8 sc. Sc2tog over next 2 sc. 21 sc.

2nd row: Ch 1. 1 sc in each st to end of row. Turn.

3rd row: Ch 1. Sc2tog over first 2 sc. 1 sc in each of next 6 sc. Sc2tog over next 2 sc. 1 sc in next sc. Sc2tog over next 2 sc. 1 sc in each of next 6 sc. Sc2tog over next 2 sc. 17 sc.

4th row: As 2nd row.

5th row: Ch 1. Sc2tog over first 2 sc. 1 sc in each of next 4 sc. Sc2tog over next 2 sc. 1 sc in next sc. Sc2tog over next 2 sc. 1 sc in each of next 4 sc. Sc2tog over next 2 sc. 13 sc. Fasten off. Sew top and side seam.

Thumb: With RS of work facing and larger hook, join yarn with sl st at ch-1 marker for Thumb.

1st rnd: Ch 1. 1 sc in same sp as sl st. 1 sc in each sc around. Join with sl st to first sc. 12 sc. Rep last rnd until Thumb measures 2½ ins [6 cm].

Next rnd: Ch 1. (Sc2tog) 6 times. 6 sts. Fasten off leaving a long end. Thread yarn through darning needle and draw through rem sts. Fasten tightly.***

LEFT MITTEN

Work from ** to ** as given for Right Mitten.

Shape thumb gusset: 1st row: Ch 1. 1 sc in each of next 8 sc. 2 sc in next sc. 1 sc in next sc. 2 sc in next sc. 1 sc in each of next 14 sc. Turn.

2nd row: Ch 1. 1 sc in each of next 14 sc. 2 sc in next sc. 1 sc in each of next 3 sc. 2 sc in next sc. 1 sc in each of next 8 sc. Turn.

3rd row: Ch 1. 1 sc in each of next 8 sc. 2 sc in next sc. 1 sc in each of next 5 sc. 2 sc in next sc. 1 sc in each of next 14 sc. Turn.

4th row: Ch 1. 1 sc in each of next 14 sc. 2 sc in next sc. 1 sc in each of next 7 sc. 2 sc in next sc. 1 sc in each of next 8 sc. Turn.

5th row: Ch 1. 1 sc in each of next 8 sc. 2 sc in next sc. 1 sc in each of next 9 sc. 2 sc in next sc. 1 sc in each of next 14 sc. Turn.

6th row: Ch 1. 1 sc in each of next 16 sc. Ch 1 (place marker for Thumb). Miss next 11 sc. 1 sc in each of next 8 sc. 25 sts. Turn.

7th row: Ch 1. 1 sc in each st and ch 1 sp to end of row. Turn.

Cont even until Mitten above cuff measures 6½ ins [16.5 cm], ending with RS facing for next row.

Work from *** to *** as given for Right Mitten.

HAT

With larger hook, ch 2.

1st rnd: 8 sc in 2nd ch from hook. Join with sl st to first sc.

2nd rnd: Ch 1. 2 sc in same sp as last sl st. 2 sc in each sc to end of rnd. Join with sl st to first sc. 16 sc.

3rd rnd: Ch 1. 2 sc in same sp as last sl st. *1 sc in each of next 3 sc. 2 sc in next sc. Rep from * twice more. 1 sc in each of next 3 sc. Join with sl st to first sc. 20 sc.

4th rnd: Ch 1. 2 sc in same sp as last sl st. *1 sc in each of next 3 sc. 2 sc in next sc. Rep from * 3 times more. 1 sc in each of next 3 sc. Join with sl st to first sc. 25 sc.

INSTRUCTIONS CONT.

5th rnd: Ch 1. 2 sc in same sp as last sl st. *1 sc in each of next 4 sc. 2 sc in next sc. Rep from * 3 times more. 1 sc in each of next 4 sc. Join with sl st to first sc. 30 sc.

6th rnd: Ch 1. 2 sc in same sp as last sl st. *1 sc in each of next 4 sc. 2 sc in next sc. Rep from * 4 times more. 1 sc in each of next 4 sc. Join with sl st to first sc. 36 sc.

7th rnd: Ch 1. 2 sc in same sp as last sl st. *1 sc in each of next 5 sc. 2 sc in next sc. Rep from * 4 times more. 1 sc in each of next 5 sc. Join with sl st to first sc. 42 sc.

8th rnd: Ch 1. 1 sc in same sp as last sl st. 1 sc in each of next 2 sc. *2 sc in next sc. 1 sc in each of next 6 sc. Rep from * 4 times more. 2 sc in next sc. 1 sc in each of next 3 sc. Join with sl st to first sc. 48 sc.

9th rnd: Ch 1. 1 sc in same sp as last sl st. 1 sc in each sc around. Join with sl st to first sc.

10th rnd: Ch 1. 1 sc in same sp as last sl st. 1 sc in each of next 10 sc. *2 sc in next sc. 1 sc in each of next 11 sc. Rep from * twice more. 2 sc in next sc. Join with sl st to first sc. 52 sc.

11th rnd: As 9th rnd.

12th rnd: Ch 1. 1 sc in same sp as last sl st. 1 sc in each of next 5 sc. *2 sc in next sc. 1 sc in each of next 12 sc. Rep from * twice more. 2 sc in next sc. 1 sc in each of next 6 sc. Join with sl st to first sc. 56 sc.

13th rnd: Ch 1. 2 sc in same sp as last sl st. *1 sc in each of next 10 sc. 2 sc in next sc. Rep from * 3 times more. 1 sc in each of next 11 sc. Join with sl st to first sc. 61 sc.

14th to 16th rnds: As 9th rnd.

17th rnd: Ch 1. 1 sc in same sp as last sl st. 1 sc in each of next 5 sc. *2 sc in next sc. 1 sc in each of next 11 sc. Rep from * 3 times more. 2 sc in next sc. 1 sc in each of next 6 sc. Join with sl st to first sc. 66 sc.

18th to 20th rnds: As 9th rnd.

21st rnd: Ch 1. 2 sc in same sp as last sl st. *1 sc in each of next 12 sc. 2 sc in next sc. Rep from * 3 times more. 1 sc in each of next 13 sc. Join with sl st to first sc. 71 sc.

22nd and 23rd rnds: As 9th rnd.

24th rnd: Ch 1. 1 sc in same sp as last sl st. 1 sc in each of next 6 sc. *2 sc in next sc. 1 sc in each of next 13 sc. Rep from * 3 times more. 2 sc in next sc. 1 sc in each of next 7 sc. Join with sl st to first sc. 76 sc.

25th and 26th rnds: As 9th rnd.

27th rnd: Ch 1. 2 sc in same sp as last sl st. *1 sc in each of next 14 sc. 2 sc in next sc. Rep from

* 3 times more. 1 sc in each of next 15 sc. Join with sl st to first sc. 81 sc.

28th rnd: As 9th rnd.

29th rnd: Ch 1. 1 sc in same sp as last sl st. 1 sc in each of next 7 sc. *2 sc in next sc. 1 sc in each of next 15 sc. Rep from * 3 times more. 2 sc in next sc. 1 sc in each of next 8 sc. Join with sl st to first sc. 86 sc.

30th and 31st rnds: As 9th rnd.

32nd rnd: Ch 1. Working from **left** to right instead of from **right** to left, as usual (see diagram), work 1 sc in each sc around for reverse sc. Join with sl st to first sc. Fasten off.

REVERSE ST DIAGRAM

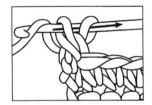 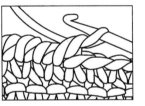

Shades of Grey Ski Band, Scarf & Bag

SIZES

Ski Band: One size to fit Average Lady

Scarf: 8 ins [20.5 cm] wide x 46 ins [117 cm] long

Bag: Approx 9 ins [23 cm] wide x 10 ins [25.5 cm] high (excluding fringe and handles)

MATERIALS

Patons Classic Wool (100 g)

Ski Band (225 Dark Grey Mix)	**1 ball**

Scarf

Main Color (MC) (225 Dark Grey Mix)	**1 ball**
Contrast A (228 Dark Natural Mix)	**1 ball**
Contrast B (202 Aran)	**1 ball**

Bag

Main Color (MC) (225 Dark Grey Mix)	**1 ball**
Contrast A (228 Dark Natural Mix)	**1 ball**
Contrast B (202 Aran)	**1 ball**

Size 4.00 mm (U.S. G or 6) crochet hook for Ski Band and Bag, size 5.00 mm (U.S. H or 8) crochet hook for Scarf **or size needed to obtain tension**. 2 metal macrame rings 6 ins [15 cm] diameter for Bag.

TENSION

Ski Band and Bag: 19 dc and 9 rows = 4 ins [10 cm] with 4.00 mm hook.

Scarf: 16 dc and 7 rows = 4 ins [10 cm] with 5.00 mm hook.

INSTRUCTIONS

Ski Band

With smaller hook, ch 31.

Foundation row: (RS). 1 dc in 4th ch from hook. 1 dc in each of next 2 ch. *Ch 1. Miss next ch. 1 dc in each of next 4 ch. Rep from * to end of ch. Ch 3. Turn. 29 sts.

1st row: Miss first dc. 1 dc in each of next 3 dc. *Ch 1. Miss next ch-1 sp. 1 dc in each of next 4 dc. Rep from * to end of row. Ch 3. Turn.

Rep last row until work from beg measures 19 ins [48 cm] when slightly stretched, omitting turning ch at end of last row. Fasten off. Sew center back seam.

Flap: With RS of work facing, fold Band flat and mark beg and end of center 20 rows along top edge of Band.

1st row: Join yarn with sl st at first marker and working into sides of dc along Band edge, ch 4. *1 dc into side of next dc of Band edge. Ch 1. Rep from * 17 times more. 1 dc where second marker was placed. Ch 4. Turn.

2nd row: Miss first dc, next ch-1 sp and next dc. 1 dc in next ch-1 sp. *Ch 1. Miss next dc. 1 dc in next ch-1 sp. Rep from * across to last dc and

ch 4 turning ch. Ch 1. Miss next dc. 1 dc in 3rd ch of turning ch. Ch 4. Turn.

Rep last row 15 times more (4 dc rem), ending last row with ch 3. Turn.

Next row: Miss first dc. (Yoh and draw up a loop in next dc. Yoh and draw through 2 loops on hook) twice. Yoh and draw up a loop in 4th ch of turning ch. Yoh and draw through 2 loops on hook. Yoh and draw through all 4 loops on hook. Fasten off.

Tassel: Cut a piece of cardboard 4 ins [10 cm] wide. Wind yarn around cardboard 35 times. Break yarn leaving a long end and thread end through a needle. Slip needle through all loops and tie tightly. Remove cardboard and wind yarn tightly around loops ½ inch [1 cm] below fold. Fasten securely. Cut through rem loops and trim ends evenly. Sew tassel to end of flap.

Scarf

With MC and larger hook, ch 36.

Foundation row: (RS). 1 dc in 4th ch from hook. 1 dc in each of next 2 ch. *Ch 1. Miss next ch. 1 dc in each of next 4 ch. Rep from * to end of ch. Ch 3. Turn. 34 sts.

1st row: Miss first dc. 1 dc in each of next 3 dc. *Ch 1. Miss next ch-1 sp. 1 dc in each of next 4 dc. Rep from * to end of row. Join A, ch 3. Turn.

Last row forms pat.

With A, work 3 rows pat, ending last row with join B. Ch 3. Turn.

With B, work 2 rows in pat, ending last row with join MC. Ch 3. Turn.

With MC, work 3 rows in pat, ending last row with join A. Ch 3. Turn.

With A, work 2 rows in pat, ending last row with join B. Ch 3. Turn.

With B, work 3 rows in pat, ending last row with join MC. Ch 3. Turn.

**With MC, work 2 rows in pat, ending last row with join A. Ch 3. Turn.

With A, work 3 rows in pat, ending last row with join B. Ch 3. Turn.

With B, work 2 rows in pat, ending last row with join MC. Ch 3. Turn.

With MC, work 3 rows in pat, ending last row with join A. Ch 3. Turn.

With A, work 2 rows pat ending last row with join B. Ch 3. Turn.

With B, work 3 rows pat ending last row with join MC. Ch 3. Turn.

Rep from ** once more.

Divide for Opening: Next row: Miss first dc. 1 dc in each of next 3 dc. *Ch 1. Miss next ch-1 sp. 1 dc in each of next 4 dc. Rep from * once more. Ch 1. Miss next ch-1 sp. 1 dc in each of next 2 dc. Ch 3. **Turn.** Leave rem sts unworked.

Cont in pat (working stripes as established) for 5 more rows. **Do not** break yarn.

With RS of Scarf facing, join yarn with sl st to first missed dc of dividing row. Ch 3. 1 dc in next dc. *Ch 1. Miss next ch-1 sp. 1 dc in each of next 4 dc. Rep from * to end of row.

Cont in pat (working stripes as established) for 5 more rows. Break yarn.

Close Opening: Next row: Pat across first side of Scarf, then second side.

Cont in pat (working stripes as established) for a further 17 rows omitting turning ch at end of last row. Fasten off.

Fringe: Cut 10 ins (25.5 cm) lengths of MC, A and B. Taking 4 strands tog, knot into fringe in every other st along ends of Scarf alternating MC, A and B throughout as shown. Trim fringe evenly.

INSTRUCTIONS CONT.

Bag

(Make 2 pieces alike).

With MC and smaller hook, ch 46.

Foundation row: (RS). 1 dc in 4th ch from hook. 1 dc in each of next 2 ch. *Ch 1. Miss next ch. 1 dc in each of next 4 ch. Rep from * to end of ch. Ch 3. Turn. 44 sts.

1st row: Miss first dc. 1 dc in each of next 3 dc. *Ch 1. Miss next ch-1 sp. 1 dc in each of next 4 dc. Rep from * to end of row. Join A, ch 3. Turn. Last row forms pat.

With A, work 3 rows in pat, ending last row with join B. Ch 3. Turn.

With B, work 2 rows in pat, ending last row with join MC. Ch 3. Turn.

With MC, work 3 rows in pat, ending last row with join A. Ch 3. Turn.

With A, work 2 rows in pat, ending last row with join B. Ch 3. Turn.

With B, work 3 rows in pat, ending last row with join MC. Ch 3. Turn.

With MC, work 1 row in pat. Ch 3. Turn.

Shape top: Next row: Miss first dc. *(Yoh and draw up a loop in next dc. Yoh and draw through 2 loops on hook) twice. Yoh and draw through all 3 loops on hook – dc2tog made. Pat to last 3 sts. Dc2tog over next 2 sts. 1 dc in last dc. Join A, ch 3. Turn.*

Next row: With A, miss first dc. Dc2tog over next 2 dc. Pat to last 3 dc. Dc2tog over next 2 dc. 1 dc in last dc. Ch 3. Turn.

Next row: Miss first dc. 1 dc in next dc. Ch 1. Miss next ch-1 sp. Dc2tog over next 2 dc. Pat to last 5 sts. Dc2tog over next 2 dc. Ch 1. Miss next ch-1 sp. 1 dc in each of last 2 dc. Ch 3. Turn.

Next row: Miss first dc. 1 dc in next dc. Ch 1. Miss next ch 1 sp. Dc2tog over next 2 dc. Pat to last 5 sts. Dc2tog over next 2 dc. Ch 1. Miss next ch-1 sp. 1 dc in each of last 2 dc. Join B. Ch 3. Turn.

Next row: With B, miss first dc. 1 dc in next dc. Ch 1. Miss next ch-1 sp. Dc2tog over next 2 dc. Pat to last 5 sts. Dc2tog over next 2 dc. Ch 1. Miss next ch-1 sp. 1 dc in each of last 2 dc. Ch 3. Turn.

Next 2 rows: Miss first dc. 1 dc in next dc. Ch 1. Miss next ch-1 sp. 1 dc in next dc. Pat to last 4 sts. 1 dc in next dc. Ch 1. Miss next ch-1 sp.

1 dc in each of last 2 dc. Ch 3. Turn. Omit turning ch at end of last row. Fasten off.

Handles: With 3 strands of MC, work 1 round of sc around each ring. Join with sl st to first sc. Fasten off.

Fold last 2 rows of Bag to inside and sew over Handles to form casing. With MC, sew Bag tog, beg and ending at last MC row of Stripe Pat.

Fringe: Cut MC 6 ins [15 cm] long. Taking 4 strands tog, knot into fringe across lower edge of Bag in each corner, then at every point where ch 1 sp occurs in pat. Trim fringe evenly.

Patchwork Purse

MEASUREMENTS

13 x 18 ins [33 x 45.5 cm]

MATERIALS

Patons Shetland Chunky (100 g/3.5 oz)

Main Color (MC) (03430 Wine)	**1**	**ball**
Contrast A (03532 Deep Red)	**1**	**ball**
Contrast B (03242 Sage Green)	**1**	**ball**
Contrast C (03022 Taupe)	**1**	**ball**
Contrast D (03031 Earthy Brown)	**2**	**balls**

Size 6.00 mm (U.S. J or 10) crochet hook **or size needed to obtain tension**. Toggle.

TENSION

13 sts and 14 rows = 4 ins [10 cm] in pattern.

INSTRUCTIONS

Front and Back (Make 2 pieces alike)

Note: To change color, work to last 2 loops on hook of first color. Draw loop in next color through 2 loops on hook to complete st and proceed in next color.

With MC, ch 9. With D, ch 23. With A, ch 12.

Foundation row: (RS). With A, 1 sc in 2nd ch from hook. 1 sc in each of next 9 ch. With D, 1 sc in each of next 23 ch. With MC, 1 sc in each of next 10 ch. Turn. 43 sc.

Next row: With MC, ch 1. 1 sc in each of first 2 sc. (Ch 1. Miss next sc. 1 sc in next sc) 4 times. (With D, ch 1. Miss next sc. 1 sc in next sc) 11 times. (With A, ch 1. Miss next sc. 1 sc in next sc) 5 times. 1 sc in last sc. Turn.

Work Chart I to end of chart, beg each row with ch 1, and noting side decs will be worked as follows: *Draw up a loop in each of first 2 sts. Yoh and draw through all loops on hook* – sc2tog made.

GUSSET AND HANDLE

With D, ch 8.

1st row: (RS). 1 dc in 4th ch from hook. 1 dc in each ch to end of ch. Turn. 6 dc.

2nd row: Ch 3 (counts as 1 dc). Miss first dc. 1 dc in next dc and each dc to end of row. Turn.

Rep last row until work fits length to measure down one side, across bottom and up other side of Purse. Work 11 ins [28 cm] more for Handle, omitting turning ch at end of last row. Fasten off.

Joining Gusset: Fold Gusset in half lengthwise. Join D with sl st in corner of Gusset. Ch 1. Working through both thicknesses, work 1 sc in each sc across first and last rows.

Joining Front, Back and Gusset: Place WS of Front and Gusset facing each other, placing seam of Gusset at center of bottom.

1st rnd: (RS). Join D with sl st in left top corner of outer edge of Front. Ch 1. Working through both thicknesses, work 1 sc in each st down to bottom, across bottom, up to top of outer edge of Front and along side of Handle. Join with sl st to first sc.

2nd rnd: Working from **left** to right instead of from **right** to left, as usual, work 1 sc in each sc around for reverse sc. Join with slst to first sc. Fasten off.

Rep for opposite side.

With RS of work facing, join D with sl st to top right corner of inner edge of Front. Ch 1. 1 sc in same sp as last sl st. Work 1 row of sc evenly along to opposite corner.

Next row: Working from **left** to right instead of from **right** to left, as usual, work 1 sc in each sc for reverse sc. Fasten off. (See Diagram on page 53.) Rep for opposite side.

Toggle loop: With D, ch 16. Fasten off. Sew to inner edge of Back to form a loop. Sew toggle on Front to correspond.

CHART I

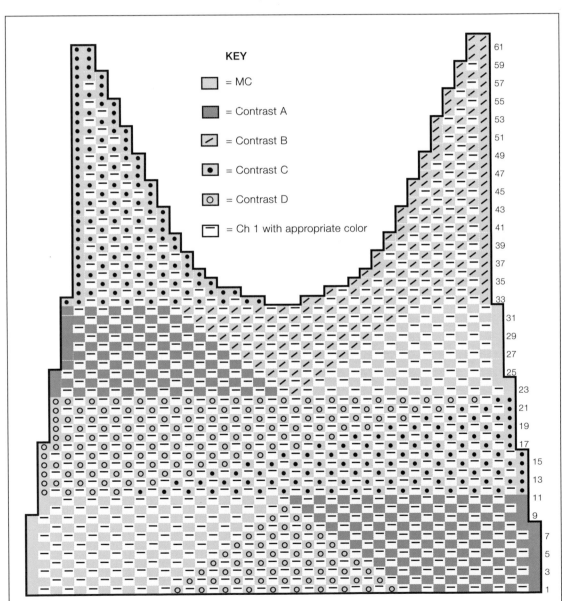

KEY

☐ = MC

■ = Contrast A

⊘ = Contrast B

⊙ = Contrast C

◎ = Contrast D

▭ = Ch 1 with appropriate color

Sheepskin Hat, Scarf, Mittens

SIZES

Hat and Mittens: One size to fit Average Lady

Scarf: Approx. 7½ ins [19 cm] wide x 50½ ins [128.5 cm] long

MATERIALS

Patons Classic Wool (100 g/3.5 oz)

Hat, Scarf and Mittens

Main Color (MC) (202 Aran)	**3**	**balls**
Contrast A (228 Dk Natural Mix or 225 Dk Grey Mix)	**6**	**balls**

Sizes 4.50 mm (U.S. 7) crochet hook for Mittens and 5.50 mm (U.S. I or 9) crochet hook for Hat and Scarf **or size needed to obtain tension**.

TENSION

13 sc and 16 rows = 4 ins [10 cm] with 5.50 mm crochet hook.

INSTRUCTIONS

Hat

With larger hook and MC, ch 76.

1st row: (WS). 1 sc in 2nd ch from hook. 1 sc in each ch to end of ch. 75 sc. Turn.

**2nd row: Ch 1. 1 sc in first sc. *Draw up a loop in next sc. Ch 5. Yoh and draw through 2 loops on hook – picot sc made. 1 sc in next sc. Rep from * to end of row. Turn.

3rd row: Ch 1. 1 sc in first sc. *1 sc in next st. Picot sc in next st. Rep from * to last 2 sts. 1 sc in each of next 2 sts. [Note: Push picot sc to the back (RS) of work]. Turn.**

Rep last 2 rows until work from beg measures 3 ins [7.5 cm], ending on a 2nd row.

Next row: Ch 1. 1 sc in each st to last 2 sts. Draw up a loop in each of next 2 sts. Yoh and draw through all 3 loops on hook – sc2tog made. 74 sc. Join A to last st. Break MC.

Reversing WS to RS for cuff turn-back, proceed as follows:

1st row: (RS). 1 sc in each of first 4 sc. *[Yoh and draw up a loop around post of next st 2 rows below inserting hook from right to left. (Yoh and draw through 2 loops on hook) twice - 1 dcfp made] 3 times. 1 sc in each of next 6 sc. Rep from * to last 7 sts. (1 dcfp around next sc 2 rows below) 3 times. 1 sc in each of last 4 sts. Ch 1. Turn.

2nd row: 1 sc in each st to end of row. Ch 1. Turn.

3rd row: 1 sc in each of first 4 sc. *(1 dcfp around next dcfp 2 rows below) 3 times. 1 sc in each of next 6 sc. Rep from * to last 7 sts. (1 dcfp around next dcfp 2 rows below) 3 times. 1 sc in each of last 4 sc. Ch 1. Turn.

4th row: As 2nd row.

Rep 3rd and 4th rows until work from turn-back row measures 5 ins [12.5 cm], ending with RS facing for next row.

Shape top: 1st row: 1 sc in each of first 4 sc. *(1 dcfp around next dcfp 2 rows below) 3 times. 1 sc in each of next 2 sts. Sc2tog over next 2 sts. 1 sc in each of next 2 sts. Rep from * to last 7 sts. (1 dcfp around next dcfp 2 rows below) 3 times. 1 sc in each of last 4 sts. Ch 1. Turn. 67 sts.

2nd and alt rows: 1 sc in each st to end of row. Ch 1. Turn.

3rd row: 1 sc in first st. Sc2tog over next 2 sts. 1 sc in next st. *(1 dcfp around next dcfp 2 rows below) 3 times. Sc2tog over next 2 sts. 1 sc in next st. Sc2tog over next 2 sts. Rep from * to last 7 sts. (1 dcfp around next dcfp 2 rows below) 3 times. 1 sc in next st. Sc2tog over next 2 sts. 1 sc in last st. Ch 1. Turn. 51 sts.

5th row: 1 sc in first st. Sc2tog over next 2 sts. *(1 dcfp around next dcfp 2 rows below) 3 times. 1 sc in next st. Sc2tog over next 2 sts. Rep from * to last 6 sts. (1 dcfp around next dcfp 2 rows below) 3 times. 1 sc in each of last 3 sts. Ch 1. Turn. 43 sts.

7th row: 1 sc in each of first 2 sts. *(1 dcfp around next dcfp 2 rows below) 3 times. Sc2tog over next 2 sts. Rep from * to last 6 sts. (1 dcfp around next dcfp 2 rows below) 3 times. Sc2tog over next 2 sts. 1 sc in last st. Ch 1. Turn. 35 sts.

9th row: Sc2tog over first 2 sts. *(Yoh and draw up a loop from right to left around stem of next dcfp 2 rows below. Yoh and draw through 2 loops on hook) 3 times. Yoh and draw through all loops on hook – 1 dcfp3tog made. 1 sc in next st. Rep from * to last 2 sts. Sc2tog over last 2 sts. 16 sts. Fasten off leaving a long end. Draw end through rem sts and fasten securely. Sew center back seam. Fold lower edge to RS and tack in place at seam.

EARFLAPS (make 2)

With A and larger hook, ch 15.

1st row: (RS). 1 sc in 2nd ch from hook. 1 sc in each ch to end of ch. 14 sc.

2nd row: Ch 1. 1 sc in each st to end of row. Turn.

3rd row: Ch 1. 1 sc in first sc. (1 dcfp around post of next st 2 rows below) 3 times. 1 sc in each of next 6 sc. (1 dcfp around post of next st 2 rows below) 3 times. 1 sc in last sc.

4th row: As 2nd row.

Rep last 2 rows 3 times more.

Proceed as follows:

1st row: Ch 1. 1 sc in first st. (1 dcfp around post of next st 2 rows below) 3 times. Sc2tog over next 2 sts. 1 sc in each of next 2 sts. Sc2tog over next 2 sts. (1 dcfp around post of next st 2 rows below) 3 times. 1 sc in last st. Turn. 12 sts.

2nd and alt rows: Ch 1. 1 sc in each st to end of row. Turn.

3rd row: Ch 1. 1 sc in first st. (1 dcfp around post of next st 2 rows below) 3 times. (Sc2tog over next 2 sts) twice. (1 dcfp around post of next st 2 rows below) 3 times. 1 sc in last st. Turn. 10 sts.

5th row: Ch 1. 1 sc in first st. (1 dcfp around post of next st 2 rows below) 3 times. Sc2tog over next 2 sts. (1 dcfp around post of next st 2 rows below) 3 times. 1 sc in last st. Turn. 9 sts.

7th row: Ch 1. 1 sc in first st. 1 dcfp3tog around posts of each of next 3 sts 2 rows below. Miss next st. 1 dcfp3tog around posts of each of next 3 sts 2 rows below. 1 sc in last st. Turn. 4 sts.

9th row: Ch 1. Draw up a loop in each st across. Yoh and draw through all loops on hook. Fasten off. Sew Earflaps to Hat as shown.

INSTRUCTIONS CONT.

Twisted cord: (Make 2). Cut 2 strands of A 23 ins [58.5 cm] long. With both strands tog hold one end and with someone holding other end, twist strands to the right until they begin to curl. Fold the 2 ends tog and tie in a knot so they will not unravel. The strands will now twist themselves tog. Adjust length if desired. Sew one twisted cord to point of each Earflap.

Scarf

With MC and larger hook, ch 26.

1st row: (RS). 1 sc in 2nd ch from hook. 1 sc in each ch to end of ch. 25 sc. Turn.

Work from ** to ** as given for Hat.

Rep last 2 rows until work from beg measures 3½ ins [9 cm] ending on a 3rd row. Break MC.

Proceed as follows:

1st row: (RS). With A, ch 1. 1 sc in each st to end of row. Turn.

2nd row: Ch 1. 1 sc in each st to end of row. Turn.

3rd row: Ch 1. 1 sc in each of first 2 sc. [(1 dcfp around post of next st 2 rows below) 3 times. 1 sc in each of next 6 sc] twice. (1 dcfp around post of next st 2 rows below) 3 times. 1 sc in each of last 2 sc. Turn.

4th row: As 2nd row.

Rep 3rd and 4th rows until work from beg measures 47 ins [119.5 cm], ending with RS facing for next row.

Change to MC and work from ** to ** as given for Hat.

Rep last 2 rows until work from beg measures 50½ ins [128.5 cm] ending on a 3rd row. Fasten off.

Mittens

RIGHT MITTEN

***With MC and smaller hook, ch 34.

1st row: (RS). 1 sc in 2nd ch from hook. 1 sc in each ch to end of ch. 33 sc. Turn.

Work from ** to ** as given for Hat.

Rep last 2 rows until work from beg measures 2 ins [5 cm], ending on a 2nd row.

Next row: Ch 1. Sc2tog over first 2 sts. 1 sc in each st to end of row. 32 sc. Join A to last st. Break MC.***

Reversing WS to RS for cuff turn-back, proceed as follows:

1st row: With A, ch 1. 1 sc in each st to end of row. Turn.

2nd row: Ch 1. 1 sc in each st to end of row. Turn.

3rd row: Ch 1. 1 sc in each of first 6 sc. (1 dcfp around post of next st 2 rows below) 3 times. 1 sc in each of next 23 sc. Turn.

4th row: As 2nd row.

Last 2 rows form ridge pat.

Cont in ridge pat until Mitten above cuff measures 2½ ins [6 cm], ending with RS facing for next row.

Keeping cont of ridge pat, proceed as follows to shape thumb gusset:

1st row: Ch 1. Pat 16 sts. 2 sc in next st. 1 sc in next st. 2 sc in next st. 1 sc in each of next 13 sts. Turn.

2nd row: Ch 1. 1 sc in each of first 13 sts. 2 sc in next st. 1 sc in each of next 3 sts. 2 sc in next st. Pat 16 sts. Turn.

3rd row: Ch 1. Pat 16 sts. 2 sc in next st. 1 sc in each of next 5 sts. 2 sc in next st. 1 sc in each of next 13 sts. Turn.

4th row: Ch 1. 1 sc in each of first 13 sts. 2 sc in next st. 1 sc in each of next 7 sts. 2 sc in next st. Pat 16 sts. Turn.

5th row: Ch 1. Pat 16 sts. 2 sc in next st. 1 sc in each of next 9 sts. 2 sc in next st. 1 sc in each of next 13 sts. Turn.

6th row: Ch 1. 1 sc in each of first 13 sts. 2 sc in next st. 1 sc in each of next 11 sts. 2 sc in next st. Pat 16 sts. Turn.

7th row: Ch 1. Pat 16 sts. 2 sc in next st. 1 sc in each of next 13 sts. 2 sc in next st. 1 sc in each of next 13 sts. Turn.

8th row: Ch 1. 1 sc in each of first 13 sts. Ch 1 (place marker for Thumb). Miss next 15 sts. Pat 16 sts. Turn.

9th row: Ch 1. Pat 16 sts. 1 sc in next ch 1. 1 sc in each sc to end of row. 30 sts. Turn.

Cont in ridge pat until Mitten after cuff turn-back measures 8 ins [20.5 cm], ending with RS facing for next row.

****Proceed as follows:

1st row: *Ch 1. Draw up a loop in each of first 2 sts. Yoh and draw through 3 loops on hook – sc2tog made.* (Pat next 12 sts. Sc2tog over next 2 sts) twice. 28 sts. Turn.

2nd and alt rows: Ch 1. Pat to end of row. Turn.

3rd row: Ch 1. Sc2tog over first 2 sts. Pat next 10 sts. (Sc2tog over next 2 sts) twice. Pat next 10 sts. Sc2tog over next 2 sts. 24 sts. Turn.

5th row: Ch 1. Sc2tog over first 2 sts. Pat next 8 sts. (Sc2tog over next 2 sts) twice. Pat next 8 sts. Sc2tog over next 2 sts. 20 sts. Turn.

7th row: Ch 1. Sc2tog over first 2 sts. Pat next 6 sts. (Sc2tog over next 2 sts) twice. Pat next 6 sts. Sc2tog over next 2 sts. 16 sts. Fasten off. Sew top and side seam.

Thumb: With RS of work facing, join A with sl st at ch 1 marker for Thumb.

1st rnd: Ch 1. 1 sc in same sp as ss. 1 sc in each sc around. Join with ss to first sc. 16 sc. Rep last rnd until Thumb measures 2½ ins [6 cm].

Next rnd: Ch 1. (Sc2tog over next 2 sts) 8 times. 8 sts.

INSTRUCTIONS CONT.

Next rnd: Ch 1. Draw up a loop in each of next 8 sts. Yoh and draw through all loops on hook. Fasten off.****

LEFT MITTEN

Work from *** to *** as given for Right Mitten.

Reversing WS to RS for cuff turn-back, proceed as follows:

1st row: With A, ch 1. 1 sc in each st to end of row. Turn.

2nd row: Ch 1. 1 sc in each st to end of row. Turn.

3rd row: Ch 1. 1 sc in each of first 23 sc. (1 dcfp around post of next st 2 rows below) 3 times. 1 sc in each of next 6 sc. Turn.

4th row: As 2nd row.

Last 2 rows form ridge pat.

Cont in ridge pat until Mitten above cuff measures 2½ ins [6 cm], ending with RS facing for next row.

Keeping cont of ridge pat, proceed as follows to shape thumb gusset:

1st row: Ch 1. Pat 13 sts. 2 sc in next st. 1 sc in next st. 2 sc in next st. Pat 16 sts. Turn.

2nd row: Ch 1. Pat 16 sts. 2 sc in next st. 1 sc in each of next 3 sts. 2 sc in next st. Pat 13 sts. Turn.

3rd row: Ch 1. Pat 13 sts. 2 sc in next st. 1 sc in each of next 5 sts. 2 sc in next st. Pat 16 sts. Turn.

4th row: Ch 1. Pat 16 sts. 2 sc in next st. 1 sc in each of next 7 sts. 2 sc in next st. Pat 13 sts. Turn.

5th row: Ch 1. Pat 13 sts. 2 sc in next st. 1 sc in each of next 9 sts. 2 sc in next st. Pat 16 sts. Turn.

6th row: Ch 1. Pat 16 sts. 2 sc in next st. 1 sc in each of next 11 sts. 2 sc in next st. Pat 13 sts. Turn.

7th row: Ch 1. Pat 13 sts. 2 sc in next st. 1 sc in each of next 13 sts. 2 sc in next st. Pat 16 sts. Turn.

8th row: Ch 1. Pat 16 sts. Ch 1 (place marker for Thumb). Miss next 15 sts. Pat 13 sts. Turn.

9th row: Ch 1. Pat 13 sts. 1 sc in next ch 1. Turn.

Cont in ridge pat until Mitten after cuff turn-back measures 8 ins [20.5 cm], ending with RS facing for next row.

Work from **** to **** as given for Right Mitten.

Elegance

Classic Evening V-Neck

SIZES

Bust measurement

Extra-Small	32	ins	[81.5 cm]
Small	34	"	[86.5 "]
Medium	36	"	[91.5 "]
Large	38	"	[96.5 "]
Extra-Large	40	"	[101.5 "]
2 Extra-Large	42	"	[106.5 "]

Finished bust

Extra-Small	35	ins	[89 cm]
Small	37	"	[94 "]
Medium	38	"	[96.5 "]
Large	40	"	[101.5 "]
Extra-Large	42	"	[106.5 "]
2 Extra-Large	44	"	[112 "]

MATERIALS

Patons Brilliant (50 g/1.75 oz)

Sizes	XS	S	M	L	XL	2XL	
Long Sleeve Version							
Marvelous Mocha (04913)	11	11	12	12	13	13	balls
Sleeveless Version							
Crystal Cream (03008)	8	9	9	9	10	10	balls

Sizes 3.75 mm (U.S. F or 5) and 4.50 mm (U.S. 7) crochet hooks **or size needed to obtain tension.**

TENSION

18 hdc and 16 rows = 4 ins [10 cm] with smaller hook.

INSTRUCTIONS

The instructions are written for smallest size. If changes are necessary for larger sizes the instructions will be written thus ( ).

Long Sleeve Version

Note: Ch 2 for turning ch does not count as hdc.

FRONT

With smaller hook, ch 81 (85**-87-**93**-97-**101**).

1st row: (RS). 1 hdc in 3rd ch from hook. 1 hdc in each ch across. 79 (**83**-85-**91**-95-**99**) hdc. Turn.

2nd row: Ch 2. 1 hdc in each hdc across. Turn.

Rep last row until work from beg measures 3 ins [7.5 cm], ending with RS facing for next row.

Shape sides: 1st row: Ch 2. 1 hdc in first st. *Yoh and draw up a loop in next st. Draw up a loop in next st. Yoh and draw through all 4 loops on hook – hdc2tog made.* 1 hdc in each st to last 3 sts. Hdc2tog over next 2 sts. 1 hdc in last st. Turn.

2nd to 4th rows: Ch 2. 1 hdc in each st across. Turn.

Rep last 4 rows once more, then 1st row once. 73 (**77**-79-**85**-89-**93**) sts.

10th to 14th rows: Ch 2. 1 hdc in each st across. Turn.

15th row: Ch 2. 1 hdc in first st. 2 hdc in next st. 1 hdc in each st to last 2 sts. 2 hdc in next st. 1 hdc in last st. Turn.

Next 7 rows: Ch 2. 1 hdc in each st across. Turn.

Rep last 8 rows once more, then 15th row once. 79 (**83**-85-**91**-95-**99**) sts.**

Cont even in hdc until work from beg measures 13 ins [33 cm], ending with RS facing for next row.

Shape neck: 1st row: Ch 2. 1 hdc in each of next 39 (**41**-42-**45**-47-**49**) sts (neck edge). **Turn.** Leave rem sts unworked.

2nd row: Ch 2. 1 hdc in each st across. Turn.

3rd row: Ch 2. 1 hdc in each st to last 3 sts. Hdc2tog over next 2 sts. 1 hdc in last st. Turn.

4th row: As 2nd row.

Shape armholes: 5th row: Sl st in each of first 6 (**7**-7-**8**-9-**10**) sts. Ch 2. 1 hdc in each st to last 3 sts. Hdc2tog over next 2 sts. 1 hdc in last st. Turn.

6th row: Ch 2. 1 hdc in each st to last 3 sts. Hdc2tog over next 2 sts. 1 hdc in last st. Turn.

7th row: Ch 2. 1 hdc in first st. Hdc2tog over next 2 sts. 1 hdc in each st to last 3 sts. Hdc2tog over next 2 sts. 1 hdc in last st. Turn.

Rep last 2 rows 1 (**2**-2-**3**-3-**3**) time(s). 25 (**23**-24-**23**-24-**25**) sts.

Sizes XS and 2XL only: Next row: (WS). Ch 2. 1 hdc in each st to last 3 sts. Hdc2tog over next 2 sts. 1 hdc in last st. Turn. 24 sts.

Sizes S, M, L and XL only: Next row: (WS). Ch 2. 1 hdc in each st across. Turn.

All Sizes: Next row: (RS). Ch 2. 1 hdc in each st to last 3 sts. Hdc2tog over next 2 sts. 1 hdc in last st. Turn.

Next row: Ch 2. 1 hdc in each st across. Turn.

Rep last 2 rows until there are 13 sts.

Cont even in hdc until armhole measures 7½ (8-8-8½-9-9½) ins [19 (20.5-20.5-22-23-24) cm], ending with RS facing for next row.

Shape shoulder: Next row: Sl st in each of first 6 sts. 1 sc in next st. 1 hdc in each of last 6 sts. Fasten off.

With RS of work facing, miss next st (center front). Join yarn with sl st to next st. Ch 2. 1 hdc in same sp. 1 hdc in each st across. Turn.

Work to correspond to first side reversing all shapings.

BACK

Work from ** to ** as given for Front.

Cont even in hdc until work from beg measures same length as Front to beg of armhole shaping, ending with RS facing for next row.

Shape armholes: 1st row: Sl st in each of first 6 (7-7-8-9-10) sts. Ch 2. 1 hdc in each st to last 6 (7-7-8-9-10) sts. Turn. Leave rem 6 (7-7-8-9-10) sts unworked.

2nd row: Ch 2. 1 hdc in first st. Hdc2tog over next 2 sts. 1 hdc in each st to last 3 sts. Hdc2tog over next 2 sts. 1 hdc in last st. Turn.

Rep last row 4 (5-5-7-7-8) times more. 57 (57-59-59-61-61) sts.

Next row: Ch 2. 1 hdc in each st across. Turn.

Rep last row until armhole measures 4 rows less than Front to shoulders, ending with RS facing for next row.

Shape back neck and shoulders: Next row: Ch 2. 1 hdc in each of first 15 sts (neck edge). **Turn.** Leave rem sts unworked.

Next row: Ch 2. 1 hdc in first st. Hdc2tog over next 2 sts. 1 hdc in each st across. Turn.

Next row: Ch 2. 1 hdc in each st to last 3 sts. Hdc2tog over next 2 sts. 1 hdc in last st. Turn.

Next row: Ch 2. 1 hdc in each st across. Turn.

Next row: Sl st in each of first 6 sts. 1 sc in next st. 1 hdc in each of last 6 sts. Fasten off.

With RS of work facing, miss next 27 (27-29-29-31-31) sts. Join yarn with sl st to next st. Ch 2. 1 hdc in same sp. 1 hdc in each st across. Turn.

Next row: Ch 2. 1 hdc in each st to last 3 sts. Hdc2tog over next 2 sts. 1 hdc in last st. Turn.

Next row: Ch 2. 1 hdc in first st. Hdc2tog over next 2 sts. 1 hdc in each st across. Turn.

Next row: Ch 2. 1 hdc in each st across. Turn.

Next row: Ch 2. 1 hdc in each of first 6 sts. 1 sc in next st. Sl st in each of last 6 sts. Fasten off.

INSTRUCTIONS CONT.

SLEEVES

With smaller hook, ch 49 (**49**-51-**51**-53-**53**).

1st row: (RS). 1 hdc in 3rd ch from hook. 1 hdc in each ch across. 47 (47-49-49-51-**51**) hdc. Turn.

2nd row: Ch 2. 1 hdc in each hdc across. Turn. Rep last row twice more.

Next row (Inc row): Ch 2. 1 hdc in first st. 2 hdc in next st. 1 hdc in each st to last 2 sts. 2 hdc in next st. 1 hdc in last st. Turn. Work 5 rows even in hdc.

Rep last 6 rows to 53 (**59**-55-**59**-61-**69**) sts.

Sizes XS, S, M, L and XL only: Rep Inc row on following 8th rows until there are 61 (**63**-63-**65**-67) sts.

All Sizes: Cont even in hdc until sleeve from beg measures 14½ (**15**-15-**15½**-15½-**15½**) ins [37 (**38**-38-**39.5**-39.5-**39.5**) cm], ending with RS facing for next row.

Shape top: 1st row: Sl st in each of first 3 (**3**-3-**4**-5-**5**) sts. Ch 2. 1 hdc in each st to last 3 (**3**-3-**4**-5-**5**) sts. **Turn.** Leave rem 3 (**3**-3-**4**-5-**5**) sts unworked.

2nd row: Ch 2. 1 hdc in each st across. Turn.

Sizes XL and 2XL only: 3rd row: Ch 2. 1 hdc in first st. Hdc2tog over next 2 sts. 1 hdc in each st to last 3 sts. Hdc2tog over next 2 sts. 1 hdc in last st. Turn.

4th row: Ch 2. 1 hdc in each st across. Turn.

Rep last 2 rows (2-**3**) times more. 51 sts.

All Sizes: Next row: Ch 2. 1 hdc in first st. Hdc2tog over next 2 sts. 1 hdc in each st to last 3 sts. Hdc2tog over next 2 sts. 1 hdc in last st. Turn. Rep last row until there are 13 (**13**-13-**13**-15-**15**) sts. Fasten off.

COLLAR

With larger hook, ch 194 (**202**-202-**210**-218-**226**).

1st row: (RS). 1 sc in 2nd ch from hook. *Ch 5. Miss next 3 ch. 1 sc in next ch. Rep from * across. 48 (**50**-50-**52**-54-**56**) loops.

2nd row: Sl st in first sc. Sl st in each of next 2 ch. 1 sc in same sp. *Ch 5. 1 sc in next ch-5 loop. Rep from * across to last ch-5 loop. 1 sc in last ch-5 loop. Turn.
Rep last row 12 times more.

Next row: Ch 5 (counts as dc and ch 2). *1 sc in next ch-5 loop. Ch 5. Rep from * across to last ch-5 loop. 1 sc in last ch-5 loop. Ch 2. 1 dc in last st. Turn.

Next row: Ch 1. 1 sc in first dc. *Ch 5. 1 sc in next ch-5 loop. Rep from * across to turning ch. Ch 5. 1 sc in 3rd ch of turning ch. Turn.

Rep last 2 rows twice more. Fasten off.

Collar Edging: With RS of Collar facing and larger hook, join yarn with sl st at bottom point of outer (shaped edge). Work 1 row of sc evenly across to opposite point. Fasten off.

FINISHING

Pin garment pieces to measurements and cover with damp cloth leaving cloth to dry.

Sew shoulder, side and sleeve seams. Sew in sleeves. Sew shorter side of collar along V-neck edge (See Diagram).

Sleeveless Version

Work Front, Back and Collar as given for Long Sleeve Version.

FINISHING

Sew shoulder and side seams.

Armhole Edging: 1st rnd: With smaller hook, join yarn with sl st at side seam. Work 1 row of sc evenly around armhole edge. Join yarn with sl st to first sc.

2nd rnd: Ch 1. Working from **left** to right, instead of from **right** to left as usual, work 1 reverse sc in each sc around. Join with sl st to first sc. Fasten off. (See Diagram on page 53).

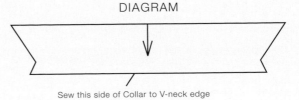

DIAGRAM

Sew this side of Collar to V-neck edge

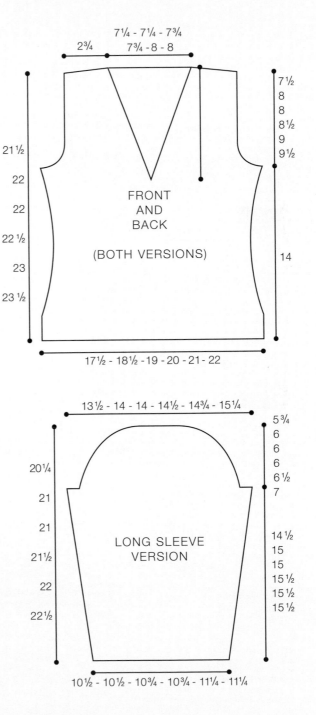

7¼ - 7¼ - 7¾
2¾   7¾ - 8 - 8

7½
8
8
8½
9
9½

21½
22
22
22½
23
23½

14

FRONT
AND
BACK

(BOTH VERSIONS)

17½ - 18½ - 19 - 20 - 21 - 22

13½ - 14 - 14 - 14½ - 14¾ - 15¼

5¾
6
6
6
6½
7

20¼
21
21
21½
22
22½

14½
15
15
15½
15½
15½

LONG SLEEVE
VERSION

10½ - 10½ - 10¾ - 10¾ - 11¼ - 11¼

Romantic Ensemble

SIZES

Scarf: Approx 7 x 67 ins [18 x 170 cm].

Skirt

To fit hip measurement

Extra-Small/Small	35	ins	[89	cm]
Medium	37½	"	[95	"]
Large	40	"	[101.5	"]
Extra-Large	43	"	[109	"]

Tank Top

Bust measurement

Extra-Small	32	ins	[81.5	cm]
Small	34	"	[86.5	"]
Medium	36	"	[91.5	"]
Large	38	"	[96.5	"]
Extra-Large	40	"	[101.5	"]

Finished bust

Extra-Small	33	ins	[84	cm]
Small	35	"	[89	"]
Medium	37	"	[94	"]
Large	39	"	[99	"]
Extra-Large	41	"	[104	"]

MATERIALS

Patons Brilliant (50 g/1.75 oz)

Scarf
Gold Glow (03023)   3   **balls**

Skirt

Sizes	XS/S	M	L	XL	
Gold Glow (03023)	6	7	7	8	**balls**

Tank Top

Sizes	XS	S	M	L	XL	
Gold Glow (03023)	5	5	5	5	6	**balls**

Sizes 3.75 mm (U.S. F or 5) and 4.50 mm (U.S. 7) crochet hooks **or size needed to obtain tension**. ¾ inch [2 cm] wide elastic for Skirt.

TENSION

Scarf and Skirt: One Motif = 3 ins [8 cm] square with larger hook.
Tank Top: One Motif = 2¼ ins [5.5 cm] square with smaller hook.
18 hdc and 16 rows = 4 ins [10 cm] with smaller hook.

INSTRUCTIONS

The instructions are written for smallest size. If changes are necessary for larger sizes the instructions will be written thus ( ).

Scarf

FIRST MOTIF

With larger hook, ch 6. Join with sl st to first ch to form a ring.

1st rnd: Ch 3. *(Yoh and draw up a loop in ring. Yoh and draw through 2 loops on hook) twice. Yoh and draw through all loops on hook – counts as cluster. *Ch 4. (Yoh and draw up a loop in ring. Yoh and draw through 2 loops on hook) 3 times. Yoh and draw through all loops on hook – cluster made. Rep from * 6 times more.* Ch 2. 1 dc in top of first cluster.

2nd rnd: Ch 1. 1 sc in loop just formed. *Ch 5. (1 sc. Ch 5. 1 sc) in next ch-4 loop for corner. Ch 5. 1 sc in next ch-4 loop. Rep from * 3 times more, ending with ch 5. Sl st in first sc. Fasten off.

Work 44 Motifs in total (2 Motifs wide x 22 Motifs long); joining sides of subsequent Motifs as follows:

2nd rnd: Ch 1. 1 sc in loop just formed. Ch 5. (1 sc. Ch 2. Sl st in corner ch-5 sp of adjoining Motif. Ch 2. 1 sc) in next ch-4 loop for corner. (Ch 2. Sl st in ch-5 sp of adjoining Motif. Ch 2. 1 sc in next ch-5 sp) twice. (Ch 2. Sl st in corner ch-5 sp of adjoining Motif. Ch 2. 1 sc) in same sp as last sc. *Ch 5. 1 sc in next ch-4 loop. Ch 5. (1 sc. Ch 5. 1 sc) in next ch-4 loop for corner. Rep from * once more. Ch 5. Sl st in first sc. Fasten off.

Edging: 1st rnd: With RS of work facing, join yarn with sl st in bottom left corner of Scarf. Ch 1. 3 sc in same sp. Work 10 sc across each of next 22 Motifs to next corner. 3 sc in corner. 10 sc across each of 2 Motifs at end. 3 sc in corner. 10 sc across each of next 22 Motifs to next corner. 3 sc in corner. 10 sc across each of 2 Motifs at end. Join with sl st to first sc. 492 sc.

2nd rnd: Ch 1. 1 sc in each sc around, working 3 sc in corner sc. Join with sl st to first sc. 500 sc.

3rd rnd: Ch 1. 1 sc in first sc. *Ch 5. Miss next 3 sc. 1 sc in next sc. Rep from * around, ending with ch 5. Miss last 3 sc. Join with sl st to first sc. Fasten off.

Skirt

With larger hook, make 64 (**72**-80-**84**) Motifs as given for Scarf, joining them into 4 circular strips each 16 (**18**-20-**21**) Motifs long.

With smaller hook, make a further 64 (**72**-80-**84**) Motifs, joining them into 4 circular strips each 16 (**18**-20-**21**) Motifs long, AT SAME TIME, joining them onto previous circular strips. There will be 8 strips of Motifs in total that should measure approx 21 ins [53.5 cm] long.

Waistband: 1st rnd: With smaller hook, join yarn with sl st to joining sp between any 2 Motifs of last strip worked (center back). Ch 1. Work 10 sc across top of each Motif around. Join with sl st to first sc. 160 (**180**-200-**210**) sc.

2nd to 7th rnds: Ch 2. 1 hdc in each st around. Join with sl st to top of ch 2. Fasten off at end of 7th rnd. Fold waistband in half to WS and sew in position, leaving an opening to insert elastic. Cut elastic to waist measurement and draw through waistband. Sew ends of elastic tog securely. Sew opening closed.

Lower Edging: 1st rnd: With larger hook, join yarn with sl st at center back of Skirt. Ch 1. Work 11 sc across each Motif around to last Motif. Work 11 (**13**-11-**12**) sc across last Motif. Join with sl st to first sc. 176 (**200**-220-**232**) sc.

2nd rnd: Ch 1. 1 sc in each sc around. Join with sl st to first sc.

3rd rnd: Ch 1. 1 sc in first sc. *Ch 5. Miss next 3 sc. 1 sc in next sc. Rep from * around, ending with ch 5. Miss last 3 sc. Join with sl st to first sc. Fasten off.

Tank Top

With smaller hook, make 15 (**16**-16-**17**-18) Motifs as given for Scarf, joining them into 1 circular strip.

Sizes XS and L only: Mark center Front of center Motif. Fold strip in half taking care to keep center Front in correct position. Mark sides at folds.

Sizes S, M and XL only: Fold strip in half. Mark sides at folds.

BACK

Note: Ch 2 for turning ch does not count as hdc.

1st row: (RS). With smaller hook, join yarn with sl st at right side marker. Ch 1. Work 74 (78**-84-**88**-92) sc across top of Motifs to other side marker. **Turn.**

2nd row: Ch 2. 1 hdc in each sc across. Turn. Rep last row until work from beg measures 11½ (**12**-12-**12½**-12½) ins [29 (**30.5**-30.5-**32**-32) cm], ending with RS facing for next row.

Shape armholes: 1st row: Sl st in each of first 8 (**8**-9-**10**-11) sts. Ch 2. 1 hdc in each st to last 8 (**8**-9-**10**-11) sts. **Turn.** Leave rem 8 (**8**-9-**10**-11) sts unworked.

INSTRUCTIONS CONT.

2nd row: Ch 2. *Yoh and draw up a loop in first st. Draw up a loop in next st. Yoh and draw through all 4 loops on hook* – hdc2tog made. 1 hdc in each st to last 2 sts. Hdc2tog over last 2 sts. Turn. Rep last row 3 (**3**-5-**5**-5) times more. 50 (**54**-54-**56**-58) sts.

Next row: (WS). Ch 2. 1 hdc in each st to end of row. Turn.

Next row: Ch 2. Hdc2tog over first 2 sts. 1 hdc in each st to last 2 sts. Hdc2tog over last 2 sts. Turn.** Rep last 2 rows 4 (**5**-4-**5**-5) times more. 40 (**42**-44-**44**-46) sts.

Next row: (WS). Ch 2. 1 hdc in each st to end of row. Fasten off.

FRONT

Work from ** to ** as given for Back, joining yarn at left side marker.

Rep last 2 rows 0 (**1**-0-**1**-1) time(s) more. 48 (**50**-52-**52**-54) sts.

Next row: Ch 2. 1 hdc in each st to end of row. Turn.

Shape neck: 1st row: (RS). Ch 2. Hdc2tog over first 2 sts. 1 hdc in each of next 7 sts. Hdc2tog over next 2 sts (neck edge). **Turn.** Leave rem sts unworked.

2nd row: Ch 2. Hdc2tog over first 2 sts. 1 hdc in each st to end of row. Turn.

3rd row: Ch 2. Hdc2tog over first 2 sts. 1 hdc in each st to last 2 sts. Hdc2tog over last 2 sts. Turn.

4th row: Ch 2. 1 hdc in each st to end of row. Turn.

5th row: Ch 2. Hdc2tog over first 2 sts. 1 hdc in next st. Hdc2tog over last 2 sts. Turn. 3 sts.

6th row: As 4th row.

7th row: Ch 2. (Hdc2tog) over first 2 sts. 1 hdc in next st. Turn. 2 sts.

8th row: Ch 2. Hdc2tog over 2 sts. Fasten off.

With RS of work facing, miss next 22 (**24**-26-**26**-28) sts. Join yarn with sl st to next st. Ch 2. Hdc2tog over this st and next st. 1 hdc in each st to last 2 sts. Hdc2tog over last 2 sts. Turn.

2nd row: Ch 2. 1 hdc in each st to last 2 sts. Hdc2tog over last 2 sts. Turn.

3rd row: Ch 2. Hdc2tog over first 2 sts. 1 hdc in each st to last 2 sts. Hdc2tog over last 2 sts. Turn.

4th row: Ch 2. 1 hdc in each st to end of row. Turn.

5th row: Ch 2. Hdc2tog over first 2 sts. 1 hdc in next st. Hdc2tog over last 2 sts. Turn. 3 sts.

6th row: As 4th row.

7th row: Ch 2. 1 hdc in first st. Hdc2tog over last 2 sts. Turn. 2 sts.

8th row: Ch 2. Hdc2tog over 2 sts. Fasten off.

FINISHING

Pin garment pieces to measurements and cover with damp cloth leaving cloth to dry.

Edging and Straps: Sew side seams. With RS of work facing and smaller hook, join yarn with sl st at left side seam. Ch 1. Work sc evenly to first point (hdc3tog). *Make a chain 10 (**10**-10½-**10½**-11) ins [25.5 (**25.5**-26.5-**26.5**-28) cm] long for Strap. **Turn.** 1 sc in 2nd ch from hook and each ch to end of ch.* Work even in each sc of body to next point. Rep from * to *once more. Work even in sc around armhole, across back neck and around opposite armhole. Join with sl st to first sc. Sew ends of straps to back.

Lower Edging: 1st rnd: With smaller hook, join yarn with sl st at right side seam. Ch 1. Work 11 sc across each Motif around to last Motif. Work 10 (**11**-11-**12**-13) sc across last Motif. Join with sl st to first sc. 164 (**176**-176-**188**-200) sc.

2nd rnd: Ch 1. 1 sc in each sc around. Join with sl st to first sc.

3rd rnd: Ch 1. 1 sc in first sc. *Ch 5. Miss next 3 sc. 1 sc in next sc. Rep from * around, ending with ch 5. Miss last 3 sc. Join with sl st to first sc. Fasten off.

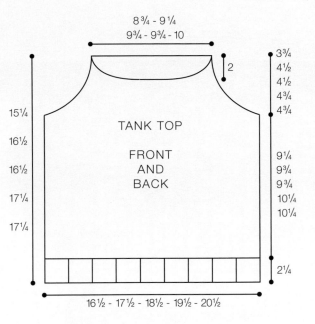

TANK TOP

FRONT AND BACK

8¾ - 9¼
9¾ - 9¾ - 10

3¾
4½
4½
4¾
4¾

2

15¼
16½
16½
17¼
17¼

9¼
9¾
9¾
10¼
10¼

2¼

16½ - 17½ - 18½ - 19½ - 20½

Elegant Open Tunic

SIZES

Bust measurement

Small	34	ins	[86.5	cm]
Medium	36	"	[91.5	"]
Large	38	"	[96.5	"]
Extra-Large	40	"	[101.5	"]
2 Extra-Large	42	"	[106.5	"]

Finished bust measurement

Small	38	ins	[96.5	cm]
Medium	40	"	[101.5	"]
Large	42	"	[106.5	"]
Extra-Large	44	"	[112	"]
2 Extra-Large	46	"	[117	"]

MATERIALS

Patons Brilliant (50 g/1.75 oz)

Sizes	S	M	L	XL	2XL	
Black Dazzle (04940)	7	8	9	10	11	balls

Size 3.5 mm (U.S. E or 4) crochet hook **or size needed to obtain tension**. ½ inch [1.5 cm] wide ribbon 1½ yds [1.4 m] long.

TENSION

24 sts and 11 rows = 4 ins [10 cm] in pat.

INSTRUCTIONS

The instructions are written for smallest size. If changes are necessary for larger sizes the instructions will be written thus ( ).

BACK

Ch 118 (122**-130-**138**-142).

Foundation row: (RS). 1 dc in 6th ch from hook (counts as 1 dc. Ch 1. 1 dc). *Ch 1. Miss next ch. 1 dc in next ch. Rep from * to end of ch. 115 (**119**-127-**135**-139) sts. Turn.

1st row: Ch 4 (counts as dc and ch 1). *1 dc in next dc. Ch 1. Rep from * to last st. 1 dc in last st. Turn. Last row forms mesh st pat. **

Rep last row until work from beg measures 16½ ins [42 cm], ending with RS facing for next row.

Armhole shaping: 1st row: Sl st in each of first 13 sts. Ch 4 (counts as dc and ch 1). *1 dc in next dc. Ch 1. Rep from * to last 12 sts. **Turn.** Leave rem sts unworked. 91 (**95**-103-**111**-115) sts.

2nd row: Ch 3 (counts as dc). *Yoh and draw up a loop in next ch-1 sp. Yoh and draw through 2 loops on hook. Yoh and draw up a loop in next dc. Yoh and draw through 2 loops on hook. Yoh and draw through all 3 loops on hook - dc2tog made.* Pat to last 3 sts. Dc2tog over next 2 sts. 1 dc in last st. Turn.

3rd row: Ch 3 (counts as dc). Dc2tog over next 2 sts. Pat to last 3 sts. Dc2tog over next 2 sts. 1 dc in last st. Turn.

4th row: Work even in pat.

Rep last 2 rows 0 (**1**-3-**3**-4) time(s) more. 87 (**89**-93-**101**-103) sts.

Cont even in pat until armhole measures 7½ (8-8½-8½-9) ins [19 (**20.5**-21.5-**21.5**-23) cm], ending with RS facing for next row. Fasten off.

FRONT

Work from ** to ** as given for Back.

Rep last row until work from beg measures 8½ ins [21.5 cm], ending with RS facing for next row.

Shape Placket: 1st row: (RS). Ch 4 (counts as dc and ch 1). 1 dc in next dc. *Ch 1. 1 dc in next dc. Rep from * 25 (**26**-28-**30**-31) times more. **Turn.** 55 (**57**-61-**65**-67) sts for Left Front. Leave rem 60 (**62**-66-**70**-72) sts unworked.

Cont even in pat until work from beg measures 16½ ins [42 cm], ending with RS facing for next row.

Armhole shaping: 1st row: (RS). Sl st in each of first 13 sts. Ch 4 (counts as dc and ch 1). 1 dc in next dc. *Ch 1. 1 dc in next dc. Rep from * to end of row. **Turn.** 43 (**45**-49-**53**-55) sts.

2nd row: Ch 4 (counts as dc and ch 1). 1 dc in next dc. *Ch 1. 1 dc in next dc. Rep from * to last 3 sts. Dc2tog over next 2 sts. 1 dc in last st. Turn.

3rd row: Ch 3 (counts as dc). Dc2tog over next 2 sts. Pat to end of row. Turn.

4th row: Work even in pat.

Rep last 2 rows 0 (1-3-3-4) time(s) more. 41 (42-44-48-49) sts.

Cont even in pat until armhole measures 3 (3½-4-4-4½) ins [7.5 (9-10-10-12) cm], ending with RS facing for next row.

Neck shaping: 1st row: Ch 4 (counts as dc and ch 1). Pat to last 14 (14-16-16-16) sts (neck edge). **Turn.** Leave rem sts unworked. 27 (28-28-32-33) sts.

2nd row: Ch 3 (counts as dc). Dc2tog over next 2 sts. Pat to end of row. Turn.

3rd row: Ch 4 (counts as dc and ch 1). Pat to last 3 sts. Dc2tog over next 2 sts. 1 dc in last dc. Turn.

4th row: Work even in pat.

Rep last 2 rows twice more. 23 (24-24-28-29) sts.

Cont even in pat until armhole measures same length as Back, ending with RS facing for next row. Fasten off.

With RS of work facing, miss center 5 sts.

Join yarn with sl st to next dc for Right Front. Ch 4 (counts as dc and ch 1). 1 dc in next dc. *Ch 1. 1 dc in next dc. Rep from * to end of row. Turn. 55 (57-61-65-67) sts.

2nd row: Ch 4 (counts as dc and ch 1). 1 dc in next dc. *Ch 1. 1 dc in next dc. Rep from * to end of row.

Cont even in pat until work from beg measures 16½ ins [42 cm], ending with RS facing for next row.

Armhole shaping: 1st row: (RS). Ch 4 (counts as dc and ch 1). Pat to last 12 sts. **Turn.** Leave rem sts unworked. 43 (45-49-53-55) sts.

2nd row: Ch 3 (counts as dc). Dc2tog over next 2 sts. Pat to end of row. Turn.

3rd row: Ch 4 (counts as dc and ch 1). Pat to last 3 sts. Dc2tog over next 2 sts. 1 dc in last st. Turn.

4th row: Work even in pat.

Rep last 2 rows 0 (1-3-3-4) time(s) more. 41 (42-44-48-49) sts.

Cont even in pat until armhole measures 3 (3½-4-4-4½) ins [7.5 (9-10-10-12) cm], ending with RS facing for next row.

Neck shaping: 1st row: Sl st in each of next 15 (15-17-17-17) sts (neck edge). Ch 4 (counts as dc and ch 1). Pat to end of row. Turn. 27 (28-28-32-33) sts.

INSTRUCTIONS CONT.

2nd row: Ch 4 (counts as dc and ch 1). Pat to last 3 sts. Dc2tog over next 2 sts. 1 dc in last dc. Turn.

3rd row: Ch 3 (counts as dc). Dc2tog over next 2 sts. Pat to end of row. Turn.

4th row: Work even in pat.

Rep last 2 rows twice more. 23 (**24**-24-**28**-29) sts.

Cont even in pat until armhole measures same length as Back, ending with RS facing for next row. Fasten off.

SLEEVES

Ch 82 (**88**-92-**98**-102).

Foundation row: (RS). 1 dc in 6th ch from hook (counts as 1 dc. Ch 1. 1 dc). *Ch 1. Miss next ch. 1 dc in next ch. Rep from * to end of ch. 79 (**85**-89-**95**-99) sts.

1st row: Ch 4 (counts as dc and ch 1). *1 dc in next dc. Ch 1. Rep from * to last st. 1 dc in last st. Last row forms mesh st pat.

Rep last row until work from beg measúres 4 ins [10 cm], ending with RS facing for next row.

Shape top: 1st row: Sl st in each of next 13 sts. Ch 4 (counts as dc and ch 1). Pat to last 12 sts. **Turn.** Leave rem sts unworked. 55 (**61**-65-**71**-75) sts.

2nd and 3rd rows: Ch 3 (counts as dc). Dc2tog over next 2 sts. Pat to last 3 sts. Dc2tog over next 2 sts. 1 dc in last st. Turn.

4th row: Work even in pat.

Rep 3rd and 4th rows 4 (**4**-5-**5**-5) times more. 43 (**49**-51-**57**-61) sts.

Next row: (RS). Sl st in each of next 5 sts. Ch 4 (counts as dc and ch 1). 1 dc in next dc. *Ch 1. 1 dc in next dc. Rep from * to last 4 sts. **Turn.** Leave rem sts unworked.

Rep last row 2 (**3**-3-**4**-4) times more. 19 (**17**-19-**17**-21) sts. Fasten off.

FINISHING

Pin garment pieces to measurements and cover with damp cloth leaving cloth to dry.

Sew shoulder seams.

Left Placket: With RS facing, join yarn with sl st to placket opening at left neck edge.

1st row: Ch 1. Work 47 (**49**-51-**51**-53) sc down side to bottom corner of placket opening. Turn.

****2nd row:** Ch 1. 1 sc in each sc to end of row.**

3rd row: Ch 1. 1 sc in each of first 4 sc. *1 sc in next sc. Ch 5. Sl st in last sc. 1 sc in each of next 3 sc. Rep from * to last 3 sc. Ch 5. Sl st in last sc. 1 sc in each of last 2 sc. Fasten off.

Right Placket: With RS facing, join yarn with sl st to bottom Right corner of Placket opening.

1st row: Ch 1. Work 47 (**49**-51-**51**-53) sc up side to neck edge. Turn.

Work from ** to ** as given for Left Placket.

3rd row: Ch 1. 1 sc in first sc. *1 sc in next sc. Ch 5. Sl st in last sc. 1 sc in each of next 3 sc. Rep from * to last sc. 1 sc in last sc. **Do not** fasten off.

Neck edging: 2 sc in same sp as last sc. Work 32 (**32**-34-**34**-34) sc up right front neck edge, 30 (**32**-34-**37**-39) sc across back neck edge and 32 (**32**-34-**34**-34) sc down left front neck edge. Working from **left** to right instead of **right** to left as usual, work 1 reverse sc in each sc around neck edge. Fasten off. See diagram.

Sew side ends of placket to body of Tunic. Thread ribbon through eyelets along placket as shown in picture. Sew in sleeves. Sew side and sleeve seams.

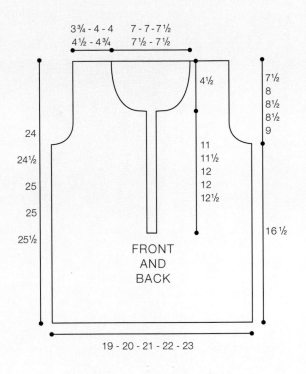

3¾ - 4 - 4
4½ - 4¾   7 - 7 - 7½
          7½ - 7½

4½

24
24½
25
25
25½

11
11½
12
12
12½

7½
8
8½
8½
9

16½

FRONT
AND
BACK

19 - 20 - 21 - 22 - 23

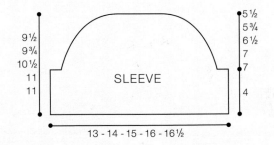

9½
9¾
10½
11
11

5½
5¾
6½
7
7

4

SLEEVE

13 - 14 - 15 - 16 - 16½

Timeless Tunic
with Matching Purse

SIZES

Bust measurement

Extra-Small	32 ins	[81.5 cm]
Small	34 "	[86.5 "]
Medium	36 "	[91.5 "]
Large	38 "	[96.5 "]
Extra-Large	40 "	[101.5 "]
2 Extra-Large	42 "	[106.5 "]
3 Extra-Large	44 "	[112 "]

Finished bust

Extra-Small	34 ins	[86.5 cm]
Small	36 "	[91.5 "]
Medium	38 "	[96.5 "]
Large	40 "	[101.5 "]
Extra-Large	42 "	[106.5 "]
2 Extra-Large	44 "	[112 "]
3 Extra-Large	46 "	[117 "]

Purse: 5½ ins [14 cm] wide x 6½ [16.5 cm] long.

MATERIALS

Patons Brilliant (50 g/1.75 oz)

Sizes	XS	S	M	L	XL	2XL	3XL	
Tunic (Beautiful Burgundy 04430)								
	6	7	7	8	8	9	10	balls

Purse (Beautiful Burgundy 04430)	**1**	**ball**

Size 3.75 mm (U.S. F or 5) crochet hook **or size needed to obtain tension**. Clasp 3½ ins [9 cm] wide. ¼ yd [25 cm] of lining fabric for Purse.

TENSION

18 hdc and 16 rows = 4 ins [10 cm].

STITCH GLOSSARY

Dcfp = Yoh and draw up a loop around post of next st at front of work 1 row below, inserting hook from right to left. (Yoh and draw through 2 loops on hook) twice - 1 dcfp made.

Dcbp = Yoh and draw up a loop around post of next st at back of work 1 row below, inserting hook from right to left. (Yoh and draw through 2 loops on hook) twice - 1 dcbp made.

INSTRUCTIONS

The instructions are written for smallest size. If changes are necessary for larger sizes the instructions will be written thus ( ).

Note: Ch 2 for turning ch does not count as hdc.

FRONT

Ch 79 (83**-87-**93**-97-**101**-105).

1st row: (RS). 1 hdc in 3rd ch from hook. 1 hdc in each ch to end of ch. 77 (**81**-85-**91**-95-**99**-103) hdc. Turn.

2nd row: Ch 2. 1 hdc in each hdc to end of row. Rep last row 0 (**2**-2-**2**-4-**4**-4) times more.

Proceed in pat as follows:

1st row: (RS). Ch 2. 1 hdc in each of next 37 (**39**-41-**44**-46-**48**-50) hdc. Miss next hdc. (Dcfp. Ch 3. Dcfp) around post of next hdc. Miss next hdc. 1 hdc in each of last 37 (**39**-41-**44**-46-**48**-50) hdc. Turn.

2nd row: Ch 2. 1 hdc in each of next 37 (**39**-41-**44**-46-**48**-50) hdc. Dcbp around post of next st. Ch 2. 1 sc in next ch-3 sp. Ch 2. Dcbp around post of next st. 1 hdc in each of last 37 (**39**-41-**44**-46-**48**-50) hdc. Turn.

3rd row: Ch 2. 1 hdc in each of next 37 (**39**-41-**44**-46-**48**-50) hdc. Dcfp around post of next st. Ch 3. Dcfp around post of next st. 1 hdc in each of last 37 (**39**-41-**44**-46-**48**-50) hdc. Turn.

4th row: As 2nd row.

5th row: Ch 2. 1 hdc in each of next 36 (**38**-40-**43**-45-**47**-49) hdc. Miss next hdc. Dcfp around post of next st. Ch 2. 1 sc in next ch-2 sp. Ch 3. 1 sc in last ch-2 sp. Ch 2. Dcfp around post of next st. Miss next hdc. 1 hdc in each of last 36 (**38**-40-**43**-45-**47**-49) hdc. Turn.

6th row: Ch 2. 1 hdc in each of next 36 (**38**-40-**43**-45-**47**-49) hdc. Dcbp around post of next st. Ch 3. Miss next ch-2 sp. 1 sc in next ch-3 sp. Ch 3. Miss last ch-2 sp. Dcbp around post of next st. 1 hdc in each of last 36 (**38**-40-**43**-45-**47**-49) hdc. Turn.

7th row: Ch 2. 1 hdc in each of next 36 (**38**-40-**43**-45-**47**-49) hdc. Dcfp around post of next st. Ch 2. 1 sc in next ch-3 sp. Ch 3. 1 sc in last ch-3 sp. Ch 2. Dcfp around post of next st. 1 hdc in each of last 36 (**38**-40-**43**-45-**47**-49) hdc. Turn.

8th row: As 6th row.

9th row: Ch 2. 1 hdc in each of next 35 (37-39-42-44-46-48) hdc. Miss next hdc. Dcfp around post of next st. (Ch 3. 1 sc in next ch-3 sp) twice. Ch 3. Dcfp around post of next st. Miss next hdc. 1 hdc in each of last 35 (37-39-42-44-46-48) hdc. Turn.

10th row: Ch 2. 1 hdc in each of next 35 (37-39-42-44-46-48) hdc. Dcbp around post of next st. Ch 2. (1 sc in next ch-3 sp. Ch 3) twice. 1 sc in last ch-3 sp. Ch 2. Dcbp around post of next st. 1 hdc in each of last 35 (37-39-42-44-46-48) hdc. Turn.

11th row: Ch 2. 1 hdc in each of next 35 (37-39-42-44-46-48) hdc. Dcfp around post of next st. Miss next ch-2 sp. (Ch 3. 1 sc in next ch-3 sp) twice. Ch 3. Miss last ch-2 sp. Dcfp around post of next st. 1 hdc in each of last 35 (37-39-42-44-46-48) hdc. Turn.

12th row: As 10th row.

13th row: Ch 2. 1 hdc in each of next 34 (36-38-41-43-45-47) hdc. Miss next hdc. Dcfp around post of next st. Ch 2. 1 sc in next ch-2 sp. *Ch 3. 1 sc in next ch-3 sp. Rep from * to last ch-2 sp. Ch 3. 1 sc in last ch-2 sp. Ch 2. Dcfp around post of next st. Miss next hdc. 1 hdc in each of last 34 (36-38-41-43-45-47) hdc. Turn.

14th row: Ch 2. 1 hdc in each of next 34 (36-38-41-43-45-47) hdc. Dcbp around post of next st. Miss next ch-2 sp. *Ch 3. 1 sc in next ch-3 sp. Rep from * to last ch-2 sp. Ch 3. Miss last ch-2 sp. Dcbp around post of next st. 1 hdc in each of last 34 (36-38-41-43-45-47) hdc. Turn.

15th row: Ch 2. 1 hdc in each of next 34 (36-38-41-43-45-47) hdc. Dcfp around post of next st. Ch 2. *1 sc in next ch-3 sp. Ch 3. Rep from * to last ch-3 sp. 1 sc in last ch-3 sp. Ch 2. Dcfp around post of next st. 1 hdc in each of last 34 (36-38-41-43-45-47) hdc. Turn.

16th row: As 14th row.

17th row: Ch 2. 1 hdc in each of next 33 (35-37-40-42-44-46) hdc. Miss next hdc. Dcfp around post of next st. Ch 3. *1 sc in next ch-3 sp. Ch 3. Rep from * to last ch-3 sp. 1 sc in last ch-3 sp. Ch 3. Dcfp around post of next st. Miss next hdc. 1 hdc in each of last 33 (35-37-40-42-44-46) hdc. Turn.

INSTRUCTIONS CONT.

18th row: Ch 2. 1 hdc in each of next 33 (**35-37-40-42-44-46**) hdc. Dcbp around post of next st. Ch 2. *1 sc in next ch-3 sp. Ch 3. Rep from * to last ch-3 sp. 1 sc in last ch-3 sp. Ch 2. Dcbp around post of next st. 1 hdc in each of last 34 (**35-37-40-42-44-46**) hdc. Turn.

19th row: Ch 2. 1 hdc in each of next 33 (**35-37-40-42-44-46**) hdc. Dcfp around post of next st. Miss next ch-2 sp. *Ch 3. 1 sc in next ch-3 sp. Rep from * to last ch-2 sp. Ch 3. Miss last ch-2 sp. Dcfp around post of next st. 1 hdc in each of last 33 (**35-37-40-42-44-46**) hdc. Turn.

20th row: As 18th row.

Rows 13 to 20 form Center Lace pattern.

Cont in Center Lace pattern, having 1 hdc less at each side of Dcfp on next and every following 4th row until the row: "**1 hdc in each of next 25 (27-29-32-34-36-38**) **hdc. Dcbp around post of next st. Pat to last 26** (**28-30-33-35-37-39**) **sts. Dcbp around post of next st. Miss next hdc. 1 hdc in each of last 25** (**27-29-32-34-36-38**) **hdc.**" has been worked.

Keeping cont of Center Lace pattern, proceed as follows:

Armhole shaping: Next row: (RS). Sl st in each of first 5 hdc. Ch 2. Pat to last 5 hdc. **Turn.** Leave rem sts unworked.

Next row: Ch 2. *(Yoh and draw up a loop in next st) twice. Yoh and draw through all loops on hook – hdc2tog made.* Pat to last 2 sts. Hdc2tog over last 2 sts. Turn.

Rep last row 3 (**3-3-3-5-5-7**) times more.

Cont in Center Lace pat until the row: "**Ch 2. 1 hdc in each of next 12** (**14-15-18-20-21-23**) **hdc. Miss next hdc. Dcfp around post of next st. Pat to last 14** (**16-17-20-22-23-25**) **sts. Dcfp around post of next st. Miss next hdc. 1 hdc in each of last 12** (**14-15-18-20-21-23**) **hdc.**" has been worked.**

Cont in pat keeping sts as placed in last row until armhole measures 3½ (**4-4½ -5-5½-6-7**) ins [9 (**10-11.5-12.5-14-15-18**) cm], ending with RS facing for next row.

Shape Neck: Next row: Ch 2. 1 hdc in each of next 13 (**15-16-19-21-22-24**) sts. **Turn.** Leave rem sts unworked.

Next row: Ch 2. 1 hdc in each hdc to end of row. Turn.

Rep last row until armhole measures 7½ (8-8½ -9-9-9-10) ins [19 (20.5-21.5-23-24-24.5-25.5) cm], ending with RS facing for next row. Fasten off.

Count over from left side edge 13 (15-16-19-21-22-24) sts. Place marker on next st.

With RS of work facing, rejoin yarn with sl st to marked st. Ch 2. 1 hdc in each of last 13 (15-16-19-21-22-24) sts. Turn.

Next row: Ch 2. 1 hdc in each hdc to end of row. Turn.

Rep last row until armhole measures 7½ (8-8½-9-9-9-10) ins [19 (20.5-21.5-23-23-23-25.5) cm], ending with RS facing for next row. Fasten off.

BACK

Work from ** to ** as given for Front.

Cont even in pat until armhole measures 7 (7½-8-8½-8½-8½-9½) ins [18 (19-20.5-21.5-21.5-21.5-24) cm], ending with RS facing for next row.

Next row: Ch 2. 1 hdc in each of next 13 (15-16-19-21-22-24) sts. **Turn.** Leave rem sts unworked.

Next row: Ch 2. 1 hdc in each hdc to end of row. Fasten off.

Count over from left side edge 13 (15-16-19-21-22-24) sts. Place marker on last st.

With RS of work facing, rejoin yarn with sl st to marked st. Ch 2. 1 hdc in each of last 13 (15-16-19-21-22-24) sts. Turn.

Next row: Ch 2. 1 hdc in each hdc to end of row. Fasten off.

SLEEVES

Ch 57.

1st row: (RS). 1 hdc in 3rd ch from hook. 1 hdc in each ch to end of ch. 55 hdc. Turn.

2nd row: Ch 2. 1 hdc in each hdc to end of row. Turn.

Rep last row 14 (10-10-6-6-6-4) times more.

Next row (Inc row): Ch 2. 1 hdc in first st. 2 hdc in next st. 1 hdc in each st to last 2 sts. 2 hdc in next st. 1 hdc in last st. Turn.

Work 16 (12-12-8-8-6-4) rows even in hdc.

Rep Inc row on next and following 16th (12th-12th-8th-8th-6th-4th) rows until there are 61 (63-63-65-67-69-71) sts.

INSTRUCTIONS CONT.

Cont even in hdc until Sleeve from beg measures 12½ ins [32 cm] ending with RS facing for next row.

Shape top: 1st row: Sl st in each of first 4 sts. Ch 2. 1 hdc in first st. Hdc2tog over next 2 sts. 1 hdc in each st to last 7 sts. Hdc2tog over next 2 sts. 1 hdc in next st. **Turn.** Leave rem 4 sts unworked. 51 (**53**-53-**55**-57-**59**-61) sts.

2nd row: Ch 2. 1 hdc in each st across. Turn.

3rd row: Ch 2. 1 hdc in first st. Hdc2tog over next 2 sts. 1 hdc in each st to last 3 sts. Hdc2tog over next 2 sts. 1 hdc in last st. Turn.

4th row: Ch 2. 1 hdc in each st across. Turn.

Rep last 2 rows 1 (**2**-3-**3**-5-**7**-9) time(s) more. 47 (**47**-45-**47**-45-**43**-41) sts.

Rep 3rd row only until there are 15 (**15**-15-**17**-17-**19**-23) sts. Fasten off.

FINISHING

Pin garment pieces to measurements. Cover with a damp cloth, leaving cloth to dry.

Sew shoulder seams. Sew in sleeves. Sew side and sleeve seams.

Bottom Edging of Front and Back: With RS of work facing, join yarn with sl st to first st of foundation ch at side seam.

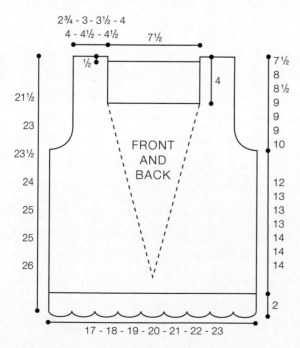

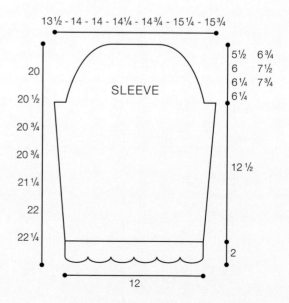

1st rnd: Ch 1. 1 sc in same sp as last sl st. *Ch 3. Miss next 2 ch. 1 sc in next ch. Rep from * to last 2 ch. Ch 1. 1 dc in top of first sc.

2nd to 6th rnds: Ch 1. 1 sc in top of dc. *Ch 3. 1 sc in next ch-3 sp. Rep from * around. Ch 1. 1 dc in top of first sc.

7th rnd: Ch 1. 1 sc in top of dc. *(4 dc. *Ch 3. Sl st to top of last dc* – Picot made. 3 dc) all in next ch-3 sp. 1 sc in next ch-3 sp. Rep from * around. Join with sl st to first sc. Fasten off.

Sleeve Edging: With RS of work facing, join yarn with sl st to first st of foundation ch at seam. Work as given for Bottom Edging.

Neck Edging: 1st rnd: With RS of work facing, join yarn with sl st to left back corner of neck edge. Ch 1. 1 sc in same sp as last sl st. Work 3 sc up left back neck edge, 19 sc down left front neck edge, 50 sc across front neck edge, 19 sc up right front neck edge, 3 sc down right back neck edge and 50 sc across back neck edge. Join with sl st to first sc.

2nd rnd: Ch 1. 1 sc in same sp as last sl st. *Miss next 3 sc. (4 dc. Picot. 3 dc) all in next sc. Miss next 3 sc. 1 sc in next sc.* Rep from * to * twice more. Working across front neck edge: 1 sc in next sc. Rep from * to * 7 times. Working up left neck edge: 1 sc in next sc. Rep from * to * 3 times. Working across back neck edge: 1 sc in next sc. Rep from * to * 7 times. Join with sl st to first sc. Fasten off.

Purse

BACK AND FRONT (make alike)

Ch 23.

1st row: 1 hdc in 3rd ch from hook. 1 hdc in each ch to end of ch. Turn. 21 hdc.

Proceed in pat as follows:

1st row: (RS). Ch 2. 1 hdc in each of next 9 hdc. Miss next hdc. (Dcfp. Ch 3. Dcfp) around post of next hdc. Miss next hdc. 1 hdc in each of last 9 hdc. Turn.

2nd row: Ch 2. 1 hdc in each of next 9 hdc. Dcbp around post of next st. Ch 2. 1 sc in next ch-3 sp. Ch 2. Dcbp around post of next st. 1 hdc in each of last 9 hdc. Turn.

3rd row: Ch 2. 1 hdc in each of next 8 hdc. Miss next hdc. Dcfp around post of next st. Ch 2. 1 sc in next ch-2 sp. Ch 3. 1 sc in last ch-2 sp. Ch 2. Dcfp around post of next st. Miss next hdc. 1 hdc in each of last 8 hdc. Turn.

INSTRUCTIONS CONT.

4th row: Ch 2. 1 hdc in each of next 8 hdc. Dcbp around post of next st. Ch 3. Miss next ch-2 sp. 1 sc in next ch-3 sp. Ch 3. Miss last ch-2 sp. Dcbp around post of next st. 1 hdc in each of last 8 hdc. Turn.

5th row: Ch 2. 1 hdc in each of next 7 hdc. Miss next hdc. Dcfp around post of next st. (Ch 3. 1 sc in next ch-3 sp) twice. Ch 3. Dcfp around post of next st. Miss next hdc. 1 hdc in each of last 7 hdc. Turn.

6th row: Ch 2. 1 hdc in each of next 7 hdc. Dcbp around post of next st. Ch 2. (1 sc in next ch-3 sp. Ch 3) twice. 1 sc in last ch-3 sp. Ch 2. Dcbp around post of next st. 1 hdc in each of last 7 hdc. Turn.

7th row: Ch 2. 1 hdc in each of next 6 hdc. Miss next hdc. Dcfp around post of next st. Ch 2. 1 sc in next ch-2 sp. *Ch 3. 1 sc in next ch-3 sp. Rep from * to last ch-2 sp. Ch 3. 1 sc in last ch-2 sp. Ch 2. Dcfp around post of next st. Miss next hdc. 1 hdc in each of last 6 hdc. Turn.

8th row: Ch 2. 1 hdc in each of next 6 hdc. Dcbp around post of next st. Miss next ch-2 sp. *Ch 3. 1 sc in next ch-3 sp. Rep from * to last ch-2 sp. Ch 3. Miss last ch-2 sp. Dcbp around post of next st. 1 hdc in each of last 6 hdc. Turn.

9th row: Ch 2. 1 hdc in each of next 5 hdc. Miss next hdc. Dcfp around post of next st. Ch 3. *1 sc in next ch-3 sp. Ch 3. Rep from * to last ch-3 sp. 1 sc in last ch-3 sp. Ch 3. Dcfp around post of next st. Miss next hdc. 1 hdc in each of last 5 hdc. Turn.

10th row: Ch 2. 1 hdc in each of next 5 hdc. Dcbp around post of next st. Ch 2. *1 sc in next ch-3 sp. Ch 3. Rep from * to last ch-3 sp. 1 sc in last ch-3 sp. Ch 2. Dcbp around post of next st. 1 hdc in each of last 5 hdc. Turn.

11th row: Ch 2. 1 hdc in each of next 4 hdc. Miss next hdc. Dcfp around post of next st. Ch 2. 1 sc in next ch-2 sp. *Ch 3. 1 sc in next ch-3 sp. Rep from * to last ch-2 sp. Ch 3. 1 sc in last ch-2 sp. Ch 2. Dcfp around post of next st. Miss next hdc. 1 hdc in each of last 4 hdc. Turn.

12th row: Ch 2. 1 hdc in each of next 4 hdc. Dcbp around post of next st. Miss next ch-2 sp. *Ch 3. 1 sc in next ch-3 sp. Rep from * to last ch-2 sp. Ch 3. Miss last ch-2 sp. Dcbp around post of next st. 1 hdc in each of last 4 hdc. Turn.

13th row: Ch 2. 1 hdc in each of next 3 hdc. Miss next hdc. Dcfp around post of next st. Ch 3. *1 sc in next ch-3 sp. Ch 3. Rep from * to last ch-3 sp. 1 sc in last ch-3 sp. Ch 3. Dcfp around post of next st. Miss next hdc. 1 hdc in each of last 3 hdc. Turn.

14th row: Ch 2. 1 hdc in each of next 3 hdc. Dcbp around post of next st. Ch 2. *1 sc in next ch-3 sp. Ch 3. Rep from * to last ch-3 sp. 1 sc in last ch-3 sp. Ch 2. Dcbp around post of next st. 1 hdc in each of last 3 hdc. Turn.

15th row: Ch 2. 1 hdc in each of next 2 hdc. Miss next hdc. Dcfp around post of next st. Ch 2. 1 sc in next ch-2 sp. *Ch 3. 1 sc in next ch-3 sp. Rep from * to last ch-2 sp. Ch 3. 1 sc in last ch-2 sp. Ch 2. Dcfp around post of next st. Miss next hdc. 1 hdc in each of last 2 hdc. Turn.

16th row: Ch 2. 1 hdc in each of next 2 hdc. Dcbp around post of next st. Miss next ch-2 sp. *Ch 3. 1 sc in next ch-3 sp. Rep from * to last ch-2 sp. Ch 3. Miss last ch-2 sp. Dcbp around post of next st. 1 hdc in each of last 2 hdc. Turn.

17th row: Ch 2. 1 hdc in first hdc. Miss next hdc. Dcfp around post of next st. Ch 3. *1 sc in next ch-3 sp. Ch 3. Rep from * to last ch-3 sp. 1 sc in last ch-3 sp. Ch 3. Dcfp around post of next st. Miss next hdc. 1 hdc in last hdc. Turn.

18th row: Ch 2. 1 hdc in first hdc. Dcbp around post of next st. Ch 2. *1 sc in next ch-3 sp. Ch 3. Rep from * to last ch-3 sp. 1 sc in last ch-3 sp. Ch 2. Dcbp around post of next st. 1 hdc in last hdc. Fasten off.

Lining: Before sewing Front and Back tog, mark wrong side of lining fabric according to Front and Back shapes with ¾ inch [1.5 cm] seam allowance. Cut out lining pieces. Sew sides and bottom of lining pieces together using a french seam (see Diagram on page 116).

Joining Back and Front: With RS of Front and Back tog, join yarn with sl st to top left corner. Ch 1. Working through both thicknesses, work 1 row of sc down left side of Bag. Fasten off. Rep for other side, leaving bottom unworked. Turn Bag right side out.

With RS of work facing, join yarn with sl st to right bottom corner. Ch 1. Working through both thicknesses, 1 sc in same sp as last sl st. *1 sc in next ch-3 sp. (4 dc. *Ch 3. Sl st in top of last dc* - Picot made. 3 dc) all in next ch-3 sp. Rep from * 4 times more. 1 sc in next ch-3 sp. 1 sc in corner of Bag. Fasten off.

INSTRUCTIONS CONT.

After joining Front and Back, fold and stitch lining along top of Bag ½ inch [1 cm] from edge. Press lining to wrong side along this stitching line. Sew Back and Front to clasp.

Handle: Ch 50. Sl st in 2nd ch from hook. Sl st in each ch to end of ch. **Do not** turn. Working into rem loops of foundation ch, sl st into each rem loop to end of ch. Fasten off.

Sew Handle to clasp.

DIAGRAM: FRENCH SEAM

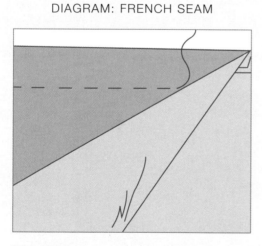

With WS tog sew a seam ½ inch [1.5 cm] wide. Trim this seam to ⅛ inch [3 mm] and press to one side. Fold fabric with RS tog along seam line and press. Stitch a seam ¼ inch [5 mm] from fold.

Spring Glamour

Retro Tops

SIZES

Bust measurement

Extra-Small	32 ins	[81.5 cm]
Small	34 "	[86.5 "]
Medium	36 "	[91.5 "]
Large	38 "	[96.5 "]
Extra-Large	40 "	[101.5 "]

Finished bust measurement

Extra-Small	34 ins	[86.5 cm]
Small	36 "	[91.5 "]
Medium	38 "	[96.5 "]
Large	40 "	[101.5 "]
Extra-Large	42 "	[106.5 "]

MATERIALS

Sizes	XS	S	M	L	XL	
Patons Grace (50 g/1.75 oz)						
Top with Rings						
Main Color (MC) (60104 Azure)						
	5	5	6	6	7	balls
Contrast A (60603 Apricot)						
	1	1	1	1	1	ball
Top with Discs						
Main Color (MC) (60604 Terracotta)						
	5	5	6	6	7	balls

Sizes 3.50 mm (U.S. D or 3) and 4 mm (U.S. G or 6) crochet hooks **or size needed to obtain tension.**

TENSION

5 Clusters and 10 rows = 4 ins [10 cm] with larger hook in pat.

INSTRUCTIONS

The instructions are written for smallest size. If changes are necessary for larger sizes the instructions will be written thus ( ).

Top with Rings

Note: Rings are worked in one piece for Back and Front.

First Ring: With smaller hook and MC, ch 16. Join in ring.

1st rnd: Ch 3. 31 dc in ring. Join with sl st in top of ch 3. Fasten off.

**Next Ring: With smaller hook and A, ch 16. Insert beg of ch from front to back into previous Ring and join in ring.

1st rnd: Ch 3. 31 dc in ring. Join with sl st in top of ch 3. Fasten off.**

(See Diagram).

DIAGRAM

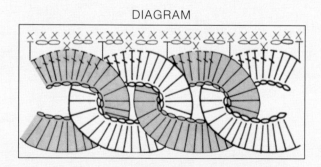

Rep from ** to **, alternating colors of Rings, until 28 (**28**-32-**32**-36) Rings are complete, joining first and last Rings in rnd.

Foundation rnd: With larger hook, working through both thicknesses of 2 Rings, join MC with sl st to dc at point where any two Rings overlap. Ch 4 (counts as hdc and ch 2). (Miss next 3 dc of next Chain. 1 sc in next dc. Ch 2. Miss next 3 dc. Working through both thicknesses of 2 Rings, 1 hdc in next dc at point where two Rings overlap. Ch 2). 28 (**28**-32-**32**-36) times. Join with sl st to 2nd ch of first ch 2.

Sizes XS, M and XL only: 1st rnd: Ch 1. 1 sc in first hdc. *(2 sc in next ch-2 sp. 1 sc in next sc. 2 sc in next ch-2 sp. 1 sc in next hdc) 13 (15-17) times. 2 sc in next ch-2 sp. Miss next sc. 2 sc in next ch-2 sp. 1 sc in next hdc. Rep from * once more omitting last sc at end of 2nd rep. Join with sl st to first sc. 166 (190-214) sc.

Sizes S and L only: 1st rnd: Ch 1. 1 sc in first hdc. *[3 sc in next ch-2 sp. 1 sc in next sc. 2 sc in next ch-2 sp. 1 sc in next hdc. (2 sc in next ch-2 sp. 1 sc in next sc. 2 sc in next ch-2 sp. 1 sc in next hdc) 4 times] (**2**-**3**) times. (3 sc in next ch-2 sp. 1 sc in next sc. 2 sc in next ch-2 sp. 1 sc in last hdc) (**1**-**0**) time. (2 sc in next ch-2 sp. 1 sc in next sc. 2 sc in next ch-2 sp. 1 sc in last hdc) (**3**-**1**) time(s). Rep from * once more omitting last sc at end of 2nd rep. Join with sl st to first sc. (**174**-**198**) sc.

Continue on page 122.

Top with Discs

FIRST RND OF DISCS

Disc One: With smaller hook and MC, ch 4. Join in ring.

1st rnd: Ch 3 (counts as first dc). 11 dc in ring. Join with sl st in top of ch 3. 12 dc.

2nd rnd: Ch 1. 2 sc in same sp as last sl st. *1 sc in each of next 2 dc. 2 sc in next dc. Rep from * to last 2 dc. 1 sc in each of last 2 dc. Join with sl st to first sc. 16 sc. Fasten off.

Disc Two: Work as given for Disc One to end of 1st rnd.

2nd rnd: Ch 1. Join with sl st to next sc of First Disc. 2 sc in same sp as last sl st. *1 sc in each of next 2 dc. 2 sc in next dc. Rep from * to last 2 dc. 1 sc in each of last 2 dc. Join with sl st to first sc. 16 sc. Fasten off.

Disc Three: **Work as given for Disc One to end of 1st rnd.

2nd rnd: Ch 1. Miss 7 sc from joining point of previous Disc. Join with sl st to next sc of previous Disc. 2 sc in first dc. *1 sc in each of next 2 dc. 2 sc in next dc. Rep from * to last 2 dc. 1 sc in each of last 2 dc. Join with sl st to first sc. 16 sc. Fasten off.**

Rep from ** to ** 18 (**19**-21-**22**-23) times more, joining last and first Discs in rnd. (See diagram on page 124).

SECOND RND OF DISCS

Disc One: With smaller hook and MC, ch 4. Join in ring.

1st rnd: Ch 3 (counts as first dc). 11 dc in ring. Join with sl st in top of ch-3. 12 dc.

2nd rnd: Ch 1. Miss 4 sc from joining point of previous Disc of First Rnd. Join with sl st to next sc of previous Disc of First Rnd. 2 sc in first dc. *1 sc in each of next 2 dc. 2 sc in next dc. Rep from * to last 2 dc. 1 sc in each of last 2 dc. Join with sl st to first sc. 16 sc. Fasten off.

Disc Two: ***Work as given for Disc One to end of 1st rnd.

2nd rnd: Ch 1. Miss 4 sc from joining point of previous Disc. Join with sl st to next sc of previous Disc. 2 sc in first dc. 1 sc in each of next 2 dc. Miss 4 sc from joining point of previous Disc of first rnd. Join with sl st to next sc of previous Disc of first rnd. *2 sc in next dc. 1 sc in each of next 2 dc. Rep from * around. Join with sl st to first sc. 16 sc. Fasten off.***

Rep from *** to *** 19 (**20**-22-**23**-24) times more, joining last and first Discs in rnd.

INSTRUCTIONS CONT.

THIRD AND FOURTH RNDS OF DISCS

Work as given for Second Rnd of Discs.

Foundation rnd: With larger hook, miss 4 sc from joining point of any Disc from Fourth Rnd. Join MC with sl st to next sc. Ch 1. 1 sc in same sp. *Ch 8. Miss 4 sc from joining point of next Disc. Sl st in next sc. Rep from * around. Ch 8. Sl st to first sc.

1st rnd: Ch 1. (8 sc in next ch-8 sp) 10 (**10**-11-**11**-10) times. (7 sc in next ch-8 sp) 1 (**1**-1-**1**-0) time. (9 sc in next ch-8 sp) 0 (**0**-0-**0**-3) times. (8 sc in next ch-8 sp) 9 (**10**-11-**12**-10) times. (7 sc in next ch-8 sp) 1 (**1**-1-**1**-0) time. (9 sc in next ch-8 sp) 0 (**0**-0-**0**-3) times. Join with sl st in first sc. 166 (**174**-190-**198**-214) sc.

Both Versions

FRONT

****1st row: (RS). Ch 4. Miss first sc. *(Yoh and draw up a loop. Yoh and draw through 2 loops) 3 times in next sc. Yoh and draw through all loops on hook – Cluster made.* *Ch 1. Miss next 2 sc. 1 sc in next sc. Ch 3. Cluster in next sc. Rep from * 18 (**19**-21-**22**-24) times more. Miss next 2 sc. 1 sc in next sc. Ch 2. Miss next sc. 1 dc in last sc. **Turn.** 20 (**21**-23-**24**-26) Clusters. Leave rem sts unworked.

2nd row: Ch 4. Cluster in first ch-2 sp. *Ch 1. 1 sc in next ch-3 sp. Ch 3. Cluster in same ch-3 sp. Rep from * ending with ch 1. (1 sc. Ch 2. 1 dc) in turning ch 4. **Turn.**

Last row forms pat.

Top with Rings: Cont in pat until work from beg measures 11 (**11**-11-**11½**-11½) ins [28 (**28**-28-**29**-29) cm], ending with RS facing for next row. Fasten off.

Top with Discs: Cont in pat until work from beg measures 9 (**9**-9-**9½**-9½) ins [23 (**23**-23-**24**-24) cm], ending with RS facing for next row. Fasten off.

Both Versions: Armhole shaping: Next row: Miss first ch-2 sp. Join MC with sl st in next ch-3 sp. Ch 4. Cluster in same ch-3 sp. *Ch 1. 1 sc in next ch-3 sp. Ch 3. Cluster in same ch-3 sp. Rep from * to last 2 Clusters, ending with 1 sc in next ch-3 sp. **Turn.**

Next 4 rows: Ch 3. *1 sc in next ch-3 sp. Ch 3. Cluster in same ch-3 sp. Ch 1. Rep from * ending with sc in last ch-3 sp. Turn. 13 (**14**-16-**17**-18) Clusters.****

Cont even in pat until armhole measures approx 2¼ (**2½**-3-**3½**-3½) ins [5.5 (**6**-7.5-**9**-9) cm], ending with RS facing for next row.

Neck shaping: *****Next row: Ch 4. Cluster in first ch-2 sp. (Ch 1. 1 sc in next ch-3 sp. Ch 3. Cluster in same ch-3 sp) twice. Ch 1. 1 sc in next ch-3 sp. Ch 2. 1 dc in same ch-3 sp. **Turn.** Leave rem sts unworked.

Next row: Ch 4. Cluster in first ch-2 sp. (Ch 1. 1 sc in next ch-3 sp. Ch 3. Cluster in same ch 3 sp) twice. 1 sc in 4th ch of turning ch 4. Ch 2. 1 dc in 3rd ch of turning ch 4. Turn.

Rep last row until armhole measures approx 6¾ (7-7½-**8**-8) ins [17 (**18**-19-**20.5**-20.5) cm], ending with RS facing for next row. Fasten off.

With RS of work facing, miss next 6 (**7**-9-**10**-11) Clusters. Join MC with sl st in next ch-3 sp. Ch 4. Cluster in same ch-3 sp as last sl st. (Ch 1. 1 sc in next ch-3 sp. Ch 3. Cluster in same ch-3 sp) twice. 1 sc in 4th ch of turning ch 4. Ch 2. 1 sc in 3rd ch of turning ch 4. Turn.

Next row: Ch 4. Cluster in first ch-2 sp. (Ch 1. 1 sc in next ch-3 sp. Ch 3. Cluster in same ch-3 sp) twice. 1 sc in 4th ch of turning ch 4. Ch 2. 1 dc in 3rd ch of turning ch 4. Turn.

Rep last row until armhole measures 6½ (**7**-7-**7**-7) ins [17 (**18**-18-**18**-18) cm], ending with RS facing for next row. Fasten off.*****

BACK

With RS of work facing, join MC with sl st to next rem sc. Work from **** to **** as given for Front omitting reference to unworked rem sts at end of 1st row.

Cont even in pat until armhole measures approx 4½ (**5**-5-**5**-5) ins [11.5 (**12.5**-12.5-**12.5**-12.5) cm], ending with RS facing for next row.

Back neck shaping: Work from ***** to ***** as given for Front neck shaping.

FINISHING

Sew shoulder seams. With RS of work facing, join yarn with sl st to first st at armhole shaping. Ch 1. 1 sc in same sp as last sl st. Work 80 (**90**-90-**90**-90) sc evenly along armhole edge. Fasten off. Sew side seams.

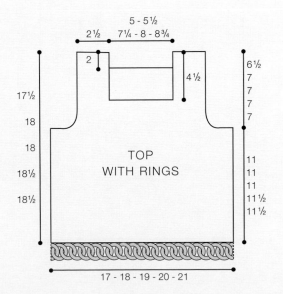

TOP WITH RINGS

17 - 18 - 19 - 20 - 21

INSTRUCTIONS CONT.

JOINING DISCS

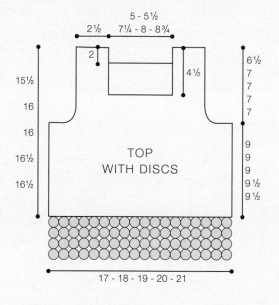

5 - 5½

2½   7¼ - 8 - 8¾

2

4½

6½
7
7
7
7

15½

16

16

16½

16½

TOP
WITH DISCS

9
9
9
9 ½
9 ½

17 - 18 - 19 - 20 - 21

White Hot Halter

SIZES

Bust measurement

Extra-Small	32 ins	[81.5	cm]
Small	34 "	[86.5	"]
Medium	36 "	[91.5	"]
Large	38 "	[96.5	"]
Extra-Large	40 "	[101.5	"]

Finished measurement under Bust (around rib cage)

Extra-Small	26 ins	[66	cm]
Small	28½ "	[72.5	"]
Medium	31 "	[78.5	"]
Large	33½ "	[85	"]
Extra-Large	35 "	[89	"]

MATERIALS

Patons Grace (50 g/1.75 oz)

Sizes	XS	S	M	L	XL	
(60005 Snow)	**3**	**3**	**3**	**4**	**4**	**balls**

Sizes 3.25 mm (U.S. D or 3) and 3.75 mm (U.S. F or 5) crochet hooks **or size needed to obtain tension**.

TENSION

22 hdc and 17 rows = 4 ins [10 cm] with smaller hook.

20 dc and 10 rows = 4 ins [10 cm] with larger hook.

INSTRUCTIONS

The instructions are written for smallest size. If changes are necessary for larger sizes the instructions will be written thus ( ).

BODY

Note: Body is worked in one piece.

With larger hook, ch 124 (**136**-148-**160**-172).

1st row: (RS). 1 sc in 2nd ch from hook. 1 sc in next ch. *Miss next 2 ch. (3 dc. Ch 2. 3 dc) in next ch. Miss next 2 ch. 1 sc in next ch. Rep from * to last ch. 1 sc in last ch. **Do not turn.**

2nd row: Rotate work around and work across rem bottom loops of foundation ch as follows: Ch 1. 1 sc in each of next 2 sc. *Miss next 2 ch. (3 dc. Ch 2. 3 dc) in next ch. Miss next 2 ch. 1 sc in next ch. Rep from * to last ch. 1 sc in last ch. 20 (**22**-24-**26**-28) Groups. Turn.

3rd row: (WS). Ch 3 (counts as 1 dc). Miss first sc. 1 dc in next sc. *Ch 3. Miss next 3 dc. 1 sc in next ch-2 sp. Ch 3. Miss next 3 dc. 1 dc in next sc. Rep from * to last sc. 1 dc in last sc. Turn.

4th row: Ch 3 (counts as 1 dc). Miss first dc. *1 dc in next dc. 3 dc in next ch-3 sp. Miss next sc. 3 dc in next ch-3 sp. 1 dc in next dc. Ch 3. 1 dc in next sc. Ch 3. Rep from * to last 2 dc. 1 dc in each of last 2 dc. Turn.

5th row: Ch 3 (counts as 1 dc). Miss first dc. 1 dc in next dc. *(Ch 2. 1 sc in next ch-3 sp) twice. Ch 2. 1 dc in each of next 8 dc. Rep from * to last dc. 1 dc in last dc. Turn.

6th row: Ch 3 (counts as 1 dc). Miss first dc. *1 dc in each of next 8 dc. Ch 3. Miss first ch-2 sp. 1 sc in next ch-2 sp. Ch 3. Miss next ch-2 sp. Rep from * to last 2 dc. 1 dc in each of last 2 dc. Turn.

Rep last 2 rows until work from beg measures approx 7½ ins [19 cm], ending with a 5th row.

Next row: (RS). (Eyelet row). Ch 3 (counts as 1 dc). Miss first dc. *(1 dc in each of next 2 dc. Ch 1. Miss next dc) twice. 1 dc in each of next 2 dc. Ch 2. Miss first ch-2 sp. 1 dc in next ch-2 sp. Ch 2. Miss next ch-2 sp. Rep from * to last 2 dc. 1 dc in each of last 2 dc. Turn.

Next row: Ch 2 (counts as 1 hdc). Miss first dc. 1 hdc in next dc. *2 hdc in next ch-2 sp. Miss next dc. 2 hdc in next ch-2 sp. (1 hdc in each of next 2 dc. 1 hdc in next ch-1 sp) twice. 1 hdc in each of next 2 dc. Rep from * to last dc. 1 hdc in last dc. 123 (**135**-147-**159**-171) hdc. Fasten off.

Change to smaller hook and proceed as follows:

1st row: With RS of work facing, miss first 16 (**22**-24-**26**-32) hdc. Join yarn with sl st to next hdc. Ch 2 (counts as 1 hdc). *Yoh. (Draw up a loop in next hdc) twice. Yoh and draw through all 4 loops on hook - Hdc2tog made. 1 hdc in each of next 85 (**85**-93-**101**-101) hdc. Hdc2tog over next 2 sts. 1 hdc in next hdc. **Turn.** Leave rem 16 (**22**-24-**26**-32) hdc unworked. 89 (**89**-97-**105**-105) hdc.

2nd row: Ch 2 (counts as 1 hdc). Miss first hdc. (Hdc2tog over next 2 hdc) twice. 1 hdc in each of next 21 (**21**-23-**25**-25) hdc. 2 hdc in next hdc. Place marker (center of Right Cup). 2 hdc in next hdc. 1 hdc in each of next 33 (**33**-37-**41**-41) hdc. 2 hdc in next hdc. Place marker (center of Left Cup). 2 hdc in next hdc. 1 hdc in each of next 21 (**21**-23-**25**-25) hdc. (Hdc2tog over next 2 hdc) twice. 1 hdc in last hdc. Turn.

3rd row: Ch 2 (counts as 1 hdc). Miss first hdc. (Hdc2tog over next 2 hdc) twice. (1 hdc in each hdc to 1 hdc **before** marker. 2 hdc in each of next 2 hdc) twice. 1 hdc in each hdc to last 5 hdc. (Hdc2tog over next 2 hdc) twice. 1 hdc in last hdc. Turn.

Right Cup: 4th row: Ch 2 (counts as 1 hdc). (Hdc2tog over next 2 hdc) twice. 1 hdc in each hdc to 1 hdc **before** marker. 2 hdc in each of next 2 hdc. 1 hdc in each of next 16 (**16**-18-**20**-20) hdc. Hdc2tog over next 2 hdc. 1 hdc in next hdc. Place marker on next st (center V-st). **Turn.** Leave rem sts unworked. 44 (**44**-48-**52**-52) hdc.

5th row: Ch 2 (counts as 1 hdc). Miss first hdc. Hdc2tog over next 2 hdc. 1 hdc in each hdc to 1 hdc **before** marker. 2 hdc in each of next 2 hdc. 1 hdc in each hdc to last 5 hdc. (Hdc2tog over next 2 hdc) twice. 1 hdc in last hdc. Turn.

6th row: Ch 2 (counts as 1 hdc). Miss first hdc. (Hdc2tog over next 2 hdc) twice. 1 hdc in each hdc to 1 hdc **before** marker. 2 hdc in each of next 2 hdc. 1 hdc in each hdc to last 3 hdc. Hdc2tog over next 2 hdc. 1 hdc in last hdc. Turn. 42 (**42**-46-**50**-50) hdc.

7th row: Ch 2 (counts as 1 hdc). Miss first hdc. Hdc2tog over next 2 sts. 1 hdc in each hdc to last 3 hdc. Hdc2tog over next 2 hdc. 1 hdc in last hdc. Turn. Rep last row 7 times more, ending with RS facing for next row. 26 (**26**-30-**34**-34) sts.

Next row: Ch 3 (counts as dc). *(Yoh and draw up a loop in next st) 3 times. Yoh and draw through all loops on hook* - Hdc3tog made. 1 hdc in each hdc to last 4 sts. Hdc3tog over next 3 hdc. 1 dc in last st. Rep last row to 2 sts.

Next row: Ch 2. Hdc2tog over 2 sts. Fasten off.

Left Cup: With WS of work facing, join yarn with sl st to center V marked st and work as given for Right Cup, reversing all shaping.

INSTRUCTIONS CONT.

FINISHING

Pin garment pieces to measurements. Cover with a damp cloth leaving to dry.

Sew center back seam.

Edging: Beg at top of Left Cup, join yarn with sl st to top st, ch 1, work 1 row of sc evenly around top edge and join with sl st to first sc.

Next rnd: Ch 1. 1 sc in same sp as last sl st. *1 sc in each of next 2 sc. (1 sc. *Ch 3. Sl st into last sc* - Picot made) all in next sc. Rep from * to end of rnd, working 3 sc in top of Cups and Sc2tog into V between Cups. Join with sl st to first sc. **Do not** fasten off.

Make tie: Make a chain 28 ins [71 cm] long. Turn chain sideways. Sl st in center "bump" at back of 2nd ch from hook and each ch to end of ch. Fasten off.

Join yarn with sl st to top of Right Cup. Make Tie as given for Left Cup.

Drawstring: Make a chain 60 ins [152.5 cm] long. Turn chain sideways. Sl st in center "bump" at back of 2nd ch from hook and each ch to end of ch. Fasten off. Thread through eyelet row and tie in center front.

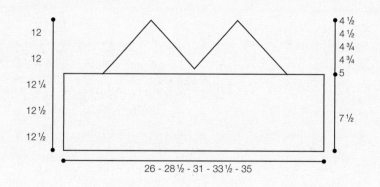

12
12
12 ¼
12 ½
12 ½

4 ½
4 ½
4 ¾
4 ¾
5
7 ½

26 - 28 ½ - 31 - 33 ½ - 35

Sweet Camisole

SIZES

To fit bust measurement

Extra-Small	32 ins	[81.5 cm]
Small	34 "	[86.5 "]
Medium	36 "	[91.5 "]
Large	38 "	[96.5 "]

MATERIALS

Sizes	XS	S	M	L

Patons Grace (50 g/1.75 oz)

Main Color (MC)

(60005 Snow)	6	6	6	7 balls

Small quantities of Contrast A (60437 Rose), Contrast B (60321 Lilac), Contrast C (60603 Apricot) and Contrast D (60027 Ginger).

Sizes 3.00 mm (U.S. C or 2) and 4.00 mm (U.S. G or 6) crochet hooks **or size needed to obtain tension**.

TENSION

25 sts and 20 rows = 4 ins [10 cm] in pat with larger hook.

INSTRUCTIONS

The instructions are written for smallest size. If changes are necessary for larger sizes the instructions will be written thus ( ).

FRONT

With larger hook, ch 104 (110**-116-**122**).

Foundation row: (RS). 1 sc in 2nd ch from hook. *Ch 1. Miss next ch. 1 sc in next ch. Rep from * to end of ch. Turn. 103 (**109**-115-**121**) sts.

1st row: Ch 1. 1 sc in first sc. *1 sc in next ch-1 sp. Ch 1. Miss next sc. Rep from * to last 2 sts. 1 sc in next ch-1 sp. 1 sc in last sc. Turn.

2nd row: Ch 1. 1 sc in first sc. *Ch 1. Miss next sc. 1 sc in next ch-1 sp. Rep from * to last sc. 1 sc in last sc. Turn.

Last 2 rows form pat.

Cont in pat until work from beg measures 2 ins [5 cm]. Place a marker at each end of last row. Cont in pat until work from beg measures 12 (12½-12½-13) ins [30.5 (**32**-32-**33**) cm], ending with RS facing for next row.

Shape top: 1st row: Sl st in each of first 3 sts. Ch 1. Pat to last 3 sts. **Turn.** Leave rem sts unworked.

2nd row: Work even in pat.

3rd row: Ch 1. *Draw up a loop in each of first 2 sts. Yoh and draw through 3 loops on hook – Sc2tog made. Pat to last 2 sts. Sc2tog over last 2 sts. Turn.**

Rep last 2 rows twice more. 91 (**97**-103-**109**) sts.

Next row: (WS). Work even in pat.

Next row: Sc2tog over first 2 sts. Pat across next 20 (**24**-24-**28**) sts. Sc2tog over next 2 sts. **Turn.** Leave rem sts unworked.

Next row: Ch 1. Sl st in each of first 4 (**5**-5-**6**) sts. Pat to end of row. Turn.

Next row: Ch 1. Sc2tog over first 2 sts. Pat to end of row. Turn.

Rep last 2 rows 3 times more. 2 sts.

Next row: Sc2tog. Fasten off.

With RS of work facing, miss center 43 (**41**-47-**45**) sts. Join MC with sl st to next st. Ch 1. Sc2tog over this st and next st. Pat to last 2 sts. Sc2tog over last 2 sts. Turn.

Next row: Pat to last 4 (**5**-5-**6**) sts. **Turn.** Leave rem sts unworked.

Next row: Pat to last 2 sts. Sc2tog over last 2 sts. Turn.

Rep last 2 rows 3 times more. 2 sts.

Next row: Sc2tog. Fasten off.

Casing: With RS of work facing, MC and larger hook, work 1 row of sc evenly across top of shaped edge. Turn.

Next 3 rows: Ch 1. Work 1 sc in each st across. Turn. Fasten off.

BACK

Work from ** to ** as given for Front.

Rep last 2 rows 5 times more. 85 (**91**-**97**-**103**) sts.

Casing: Next 4 rows: Ch 1. 1 sc in each st across. Fasten off.

FINISHING

Sew side seams above markers. Fold casing in half to WS and sew in position. Mark center point of neck edge on Front.

Large Flowers (Make 1 each with A, B and C).

With smaller hook, ch 3. Join with sl st to first ch to form ring.

1st rnd: (Ch 3. 1 dc in ring. Ch 3. Sl st in ring) 5 times. Fasten off leaving an end approx 6 ins [15 cm] long to sew Flower to garment.

Small Flowers (Make 8 each with A, B and C).

With smaller hook, ch 3.

1st rnd: [1 hdc. (Ch 2. Sl st. Ch 2. 1 hdc) twice. Ch 2. Sl st] all in 3rd ch from hook. Fasten off leaving an end approx 6 ins [15 cm] long to sew Flower to garment.

LEAF (Make 12)

With smaller hook and D, ch 8.

Sl st in 2nd ch from hook. 1 sc in next ch. 1 hdc in next ch. 1 dc in next ch. 1 hdc in next ch. 1 sc in next ch. Sl st in last ch. Fasten off leaving an end approx 6 ins [15 cm] long to sew Leaf to garment.

Sew clusters of 3 Small Flowers and 2 Leaves at each bottom corner of garment. Sew cluster of 3 Large Flowers, 4 Small Flowers and 2 Leaves at center front. Alternate rem 8 Small Flowers on either side of center front cluster. Sew rem 2 Leaves at each side.

Neck Tie: With larger hook, make a chain 64 (**66**-66-**68**) ins [162.5 (**167.5**-167.5-**172.5**) cm] long. Turn chain sideways. Sl st in center 'bump' at back of 2nd ch from hook. Sl st in next bump and each bump to end of ch. Fasten off.

Beg at center front marker, thread Neck Tie through Front and Back casings leaving approx 8 ins [20.5 cm] for each shoulder strap. Try garment on and gather casings as desired. Secure shoulder straps at each end. Tie into bow as illustrated.

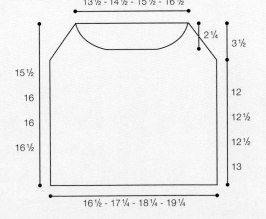

Lacy Tunic and Purse

SIZES

Bust measurement

Extra-Small	32 ins	[81.5 cm]	
Small	34 "	[86.5 "]	
Medium	36 "	[91.5 "]	
Large	38 "	[96.5 "]	
Extra-Large	40 "	[101.5 "]	

Finished bust measurement

Extra-Small	34 ins	[86.5 cm]	
Small	36 "	[91.5 "]	
Medium	38 "	[96.5 "]	
Large	40 "	[101.5 "]	
Extra-Large	42 "	[106.5 "]	

Purse: Approx 7 x 10½ ins [18 x 26.5 cm].

STITCH GLOSSARY

Sc2tog = Draw up a loop in each of next 2 sc. Yoh and draw through all 3 loops on hook - Sc2tog made.

MATERIALS

Patons Grace (50 g/1.75 oz)

Sizes	XS	S	M	L	XL	
Tunic						
60130 (Sky)	**11**	**12**	**14**	**15**	**16**	balls
Purse						
60130 (Sky)			**3balls**			

Size 3.25 mm (U.S. D or 3) crochet hook **or size needed to obtain tension**. 1 zipper 10 ins [25 cm] long, 2 pipe-cleaners and ¼ yrd [0.3 m] of lining fabric for Purse.

TENSION

8½ V-sts and 12 rows = 4 ins [10 cm]
1 Motif = 3½ ins [9 cm] square.

INSTRUCTIONS

The instructions are written for smallest size. If changes are necessary for larger sizes the instructions will be written thus ( ).

MOTIF [make 10 (**10**-11-**11**-12)]

Ch 8. Join in ring.

1st rnd: Ch 1. 15 sc in rnd. Join with sl st in first sc.

2nd rnd: Ch 6 (counts as dc and ch 3). *Miss next sc. 1 dc in next sc. Ch 3. Rep from * 6 times more. Join with sl st in 3rd ch of ch 6.

3rd rnd: Ch 1. *(1 sc. 1 hdc. 1 dc. 1 hdc. 1 sc) all in next ch-3 sp. Rep from * around. Join with sl st in first sc.

4th rnd: *Ch 5. (Miss next sc, hdc, dc, hdc). 1 sc in next sc. Rep from * around. Join with sl st in first ch of ch 5.

5th rnd: Ch 1. *(1 sc. 1 hdc. 3 dc. 1 hdc. 1 sc) all in next ch-5 sp. Rep from * around. Join with sl st in first sc.

6th rnd: Sl st in next hdc. Ch 1. 1 sc in same sp as last sl st. Ch 4. *Miss next 2 dc. 1 sc in next dc. Ch 4. (Miss next hdc, 2 sc). 1 sc in next hdc. Ch 4. Miss next 2 dc. 1 sc in next dc**. Ch 7. (Miss next hdc, 2 sc). 1 sc in next hdc. Ch 4. Rep from * twice more, then from * to ** once. Ch 7. Sl st in first sc.

7th rnd: Ch 1. (4 sc in next ch-4 sp) 3 times. *(3 sc. Ch 2. 3 sc) in next corner ch-7 sp. (4 sc in next ch-4 sp) 3 times. Rep from * twice more. (3 sc. Ch 2. 3 sc) in next corner ch-7 sp. Join with sl st to first sc. Fasten off.

JOINING MOTIFS:

Sizes XS, M and XL only: Place 2 motifs with RS facing tog. Working through both thicknessess, proceed as follows: Join yarn with sl st to any corner ch. Ch 1. 1 sc in same sp as last sl st. (Ch 1. Miss next sc. 1 sc in next sc) 10 times. Fasten off.

Sizes S and L only: With RS of 2 motifs facing, proceed as follows: join yarn with sl st to any corner ch of First motif. Ch 1. Sl st to corner ch of second motif. *Ch 2. Miss next sc of first motif. Sl st in next sc. Ch 2. Miss next sc of second motif. Sl st in next sc. Rep from * to corner sc of both motifs.
Fasten off.

Foundation rnd for Body: Size XS only: With RS of work facing, join yarn with sl st to any motif corner sc. Ch 1. 1 sc in same sp as last sl st. *Work 21 sc across top of motif. 1 sc in joining sp between motifs. Rep from * around. Join with sl st to first sc. 220 sc.

Sizes M and XL only: With RS of work facing, join yarn with sl st to any motif corner sc. Ch 1. 1 sc in same sp as last sl st. Work 20 sc across top of first motif. [(1 sc in joining sp between motifs. Work 21 sc across top of next motif) (4-1) time(s). 2 sc in joining sp between motifs. Work 21 sc across top of next motif] (2-4) times. (1 sc in joining sp between motifs. Work 21 sc across top of next motif) (0-3) times. 1 sc in joining sp between motifs. Join with sl st to first sc. (244-268) sc.

Sizes S and L only: With RS of work facing, join yarn with sl st to any corner sc. Ch 1. 1 sc in same sp as last sl st. Work 20 sc across top of first motif. [(2 sc in joining sp between motifs. Work 21 sc across top of next motif) (4-2) times. 3 sc in joining sp between motifs. Work 21 sc across top of next motif] (1-3) time(s). (2 sc in joining sp between motifs. Work 21 sc across top of next motif) (4-1) time(s). (3-2) sc in joining sp between motifs. Join with sl st to first sc. (232-256) sc.

FRONT

All Sizes: **1st row: (RS). Ch 3 (counts as dc). Miss next sc. [(1 dc. Ch 1. 1 dc) all in next sc - V-st made. Miss next 2 sc] 35 (37-39-41-43) times. V-st in next sc. Miss next sc. 1 dc in next sc. Turn. Leave rem sts unworked. 36 (38-40-42-44) V-sts.

2nd row: Ch 3 (counts as dc). V-st in each V-st to end of row. 1 dc in top of turning ch. Turn. Last row forms pat.

Cont in pat until work from foundation rnd measures 13 ins [33 cm], ending with RS facing for next row.

Armhole shaping: 1st row: Sl st in first dc. (Sl st in next dc, ch-1 sp, dc) 3 times. Sl st in next dc. Ch 3 (counts as dc). Miss next ch-1 sp and dc. V-st in each V-st to last 4 V-sts. 1 dc in next dc of next V-st. Turn. Leave rem sts unworked.

2nd row: Ch 3. 1 dc in ch-1 sp of next V-st. V-st in each V-st to last V-st. 1 dc in ch-1 sp of last V-st. 1 dc in top of turning ch. Turn.

3rd row: Ch 3. Miss first 2 dc. V st in each V-st to last dc. Miss last dc. 1 dc in top of turning ch. Turn. 26 (28-30-32-34) V-sts.**
Work 3 (3-3-5-5) rows even in pat.

V-neck shaping: ***1st row: Ch 3. V-st in each of next 12 (13-14-14-15) V-sts. 1 dc in ch-1 sp of next V-st. Turn. Leave rem sts unworked.

2nd row: Ch 3. 1 dc in ch-1 sp of next V-st. V-st in each V-st to end of row. 1 dc in top of turning ch. Turn.

INSTRUCTIONS CONT.

3rd row: Ch 3. V-st in each V-st to last dc. Miss last dc. 1 dc in top of turning ch. **Turn.**

Rep 2nd and 3rd rows until there are 6 (7-8-9-10) V-sts.

Cont even in pat until armhole measures 7½ (7½-8-8½-8½) ins [19 (19-20.5-20.5-21.5) cm], ending with RS facing for next row. Fasten off.***

With **WS** of work facing, join yarn to top of turning ch and work from *** to *** as given above for Right Front, noting RS rows become WS.

BACK

Work from ** to ** as given for Front omitting references to leave rem sts unworked.

Cont even in pat until armhole measures 2 rows less than Front, ending with RS facing for next row.

Back neck shaping: Next row: Ch 3. V-st in each of next 6 (7-8-9-10) V-sts. 1 dc in next dc of next V-st. **Turn.**

Leave rem sts unworked.

Next row: Ch 3. V-st in each V-st to end of row. 1 dc in top of turning ch. Fasten off.

With **WS** of work facing, join yarn with sl st to top of turning ch. Ch 3. V-st in each of next 6 (7-

8-9-10) V-sts. 1 dc in first dc of next V-st. **Turn.** Leave rem sts unworked.

Next row: Ch 3. V-st in each V-st to end of row. 1 dc in top of turning ch. Fasten off.

SLEEVES

Make 3 Motifs.

Join Motifs in a row as given for Size S of Front.

Foundation row: With RS of work facing, join yarn with sl st to right corner sc. Ch 1. 1 sc in same sp as last sl st. Work 23 sc across top of first motif. (4 sc in joining sp between motifs. Work 21 sc across top of next motif) twice. Turn. 68 sc.

Next row: (WS). Ch 3 (counts as dc). (Miss next sc. V-st in next sc. Miss next sc) 26 times. 1 dc in last sc. Turn. 26 V-sts.

2nd row: Ch 3 (counts as dc). V-st in each V-st to end of row. 1 dc in top of turning ch. Turn.

Last row forms pat.

Rep last row 13 (3-3-3-3) times more.

Proceed as follows:

1st row: (RS). Ch 3. 1 dc in first dc. V-st in each V-st to end of row. 2 dc in top of ch 3. Turn.

2nd row: Ch 3. Miss first dc. 1 dc in next dc. V-st in each V-st to last dc. 1 dc in last dc. 1 dc in top of turning ch. Turn.

3rd row: Ch 3. Miss first dc. V-st in next dc. V-st in each V-st to last dc. V-st in last dc. 1 dc in top of turning ch. Turn.

4th row: Ch 3. V-st in each V-st to end of row. 1 dc in top of turning ch. Turn. 30 V-sts. Rep last row 10 (**8**-4-**2**-2) times more.

Sizes S, M, L and XL only: Rep last (**12**-8-**6**-6) rows (**1**-2-**3**-3) time(s) more. (**30**-32-**34**-34) V-sts.

All Sizes: Shape Top: 1st row: Sl st in first dc. (Sl st in next dc, ch-1 sp, dc) twice. Sl st in next dc. Ch 3 (counts as dc). Miss next ch-1 sp and dc. V-st in each V-st to last 3 V-sts. Miss next dc and ch-1 sp of next V-st. 1 dc in next dc of same V-st. **Turn.** Leave rem sts unworked.

2nd row: Ch 3. 1 dc in ch-1 sp of next V-st. V-st in each V-st to last V-st. 1 dc in ch-1 sp of last V-st. 1 dc in top of turning ch. Turn.

3rd row: Ch 3. Miss first 2 dc. V-st in each V-st to last dc. Miss last dc. 1 dc in top of turning ch. Turn. Rep 2nd and 3rd rows until there are 6 V-sts. Fasten off.

FINISHING

V-Neck Edging: Sew right shoulder seam. With RS of work facing, join yarn with sl st to corner of left front neck edge. Ch 1. Work 34 (**34**-37-**37**-40) sc down left front V-neck edge. Work Sc2tog at bottom point of V-neck. Work 34 (**34**-37-**37**-40) sc up right front V-neck edge and 4 sc down right back neck edge, 38 sc across back neck edge and 4 sc up left back neck edge. Fasten off.

Sew left shoulder seam. Sew in sleeves. Sew side and sleeve seams.

Body Edging: With RS of work facing, join yarn with sl st to any corner sc of Motif.

Work as given for Foundation rnd for Body for appropriate size, to last 2 sts. (2 sc in next sc) twice. Join with sl st in first sc. 220 (**232**-244-**256**-268) sc.

Next rnd: Ch 1. 1 sc in same sp as last sl st. *Miss next 2 sc. (2 dc. Ch 3. *Sl st in top of dc -* Picot made. 3 dc) all in next sc. Miss next 2 sc. 1 sc in next sc. Rep from * around, ending with 1 sc in last sc. Join with sl st in first sc. Fasten off.

Sleeve Edging: With RS of work facing, join yarn with sl st to corner sc of first Motif.

Work as given for Foundation row for Sleeve, working (sc2tog) twice evenly around. Join with sl st in first sc. 66 sc.

Next rnd: Ch 1. 1 sc in same sp as last sl st. *Miss next 2 sc. (2 dc. Picot. 3 dc) in next sc. Miss next 2 sc. 1 sc in next sc. Rep from * around. Join with sl st in first sc. Fasten off.

INSTRUCTIONS CONT.

Purse

Make 12 motifs.

Join 3 motifs in row as follows: Place 2 motifs with RS facing tog. Join yarn with sl st to any corner ch sp. Ch 1. 1 sc in same sp as last sl st. (Ch 1. Miss next sc. 1 sc in next sc) 11 times. Fasten off.

Join 2 rows for Front or Back in same manner as given for joining Motifs.

Note: Ch 2 does not count as st.

Gusset and bottom: (worked in one piece).

Ch 4.

1st row: (RS). 1 hdc in 3rd ch from hook. 1 hdc in next ch. Ch 2. Turn.

2nd row: 1 hdc in each of next 2 hdc. Ch 2. Turn.

3rd row: 2 hdc in each of next 2 hdc. Ch 2. Turn.

4th to 6th rows: 1 hdc in each hdc to end of row. Ch 2. Turn.

7th row: 2 hdc in first hdc. 1 hdc in each hdc to last hdc. 2 hdc in last hdc. Ch 2. Turn.

8th to 11th rows: As 4th to 7th rows.

12th row: 1 hdc in each hdc to end of row. Ch 2. Turn.

Rep last row until work from beg measures 14 ins [35.5 cm], ending with RS facing for next row.

Next row: (Yoh and draw up a loop in next st) twice. Yoh and draw through all loops on hook -

Hdc2tog made. 1 hdc in each hdc to last 2 hdc. Hdc2tog over last 2 hdc. Ch 2. Turn.

Next 3 rows: 1 hdc in each st to end of row. Ch 2. Turn.

Next 2 rows: Hdc2tog over first 2 sts. 1 hdc in each hdc to last 2 sts. Hdc2tog over last 2 sts. Ch 2. **Turn.** Fasten off at end of last row.

Lining: Before joining Front, Back and sides tog, mark WS of lining according to the shape of each piece with ¾ inch [2 cm] seam allowance on side and bottom edges and ½ inch [1.5 cm] seam allowance to top edges. Cut out lining pieces. Sew bottom seam of Front, Back and sides tog using french seam (see diagram). Sew sides using french seam. Stitch along top of Front, Back and sides lining ½ inch [1.5 cm] from edge. Press lining to WS along this stitching line.

Joining Front, Back and Gusset: With WS of Front and Gusset tog, join yarn with sl st to top left corner of Front. Ch 1. Working through both thicknessess, work 1 row of sc down left side of Front, across bottom and up right side of Front. **Do not** turn.

Next row: Working from **left** to right instead of from **right** to left as usual work 1 reverse sc in each sc to end of row. Fasten off. (see diagram). Repeat for Back.

HANDLES (make 2).

Ch 80.

1st row: (RS). 1 hdc in 3rd ch from hook. 1 hdc in each ch to end of ch. Turn.

Next 3 rows: Ch 2. 1 hdc in each hdc to end of row. Turn.

Fold Handle lengthwise and insert pipecleaner, working through both thicknessess, work 1 sc in each hdc and foundation ch to end of row. Fasten off.

Sew handles to Front and Back as shown. Sew in zipper.

DIAGRAM: FRENCH SEAM

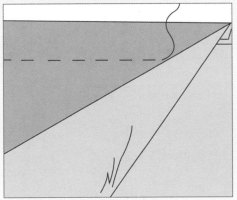

With WS tog sew a seam ½ ins [1.5 cm] wide. Trim this seam to ⅛ inch [3 mm] and press to one side. Fold fabric with RS tog along seam line and press. Stitch a seam ¼ inch [5 mm] from fold.

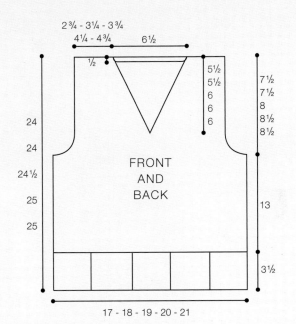

2 ¾ - 3 ¼ - 3 ¾
4 ¼ - 4 ¾ 6 ½
½
5 ½
5 ½
6
6
6
7 ½
7 ½
8
8 ½
8 ½
24
24
24 ½
25
25
13
3 ½

FRONT AND BACK

17 - 18 - 19 - 20 - 21

DIAGRAM: REVERSE SC

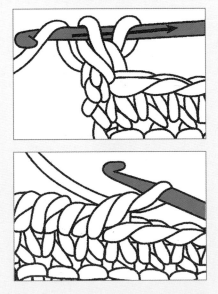

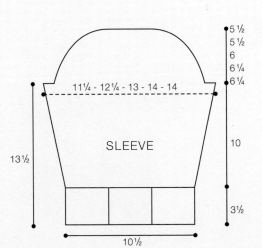

5 ½
5 ½
6
6 ¼
6 ¼
11 ¼ - 12 ¼ - 13 - 14 - 14
10
13 ½
3 ½

SLEEVE

10 ½

Open-work Cardigan

SIZES

Bust measurement

Small	30-32	ins	[76-81	cm]	
Medium	34-36	"	[86-91	"	]
Large	38-40	"	[97-102	"	]

Finished bust

Small	37	ins	[94	cm]	
Medium	39	"	[99	"	]
Large	43	"	[109	"	]

MATERIALS

Patons Grace (50 g/1.75 oz)

Sizes	S	M	L	
60409 (Ruby)	9	10	11	**balls**

Size 3.50 mm (U.S. E or 4) crochet hook **or size needed to obtain tension**. 1 button or 2.25 mm (U.S. B or 1) crochet hook for crocheted button.

TENSION

20 dc and 9 rows = 4 ins [10 cm]

INSTRUCTIONS

The instructions are written for smallest size. If changes are necessary for larger sizes the instructions will be written thus ( ).

RIGHT FRONT

Ch 51 (53**-59).

1st row: (RS). 1 dc in 4th ch from hook. 1 dc in each of next 14 (**15**-18) ch. *Miss next 2 ch. *5 dc in next ch* - shell made. Ch 2. Miss next 3 ch.* 1 dc in each of next 5 ch. Rep from * to * once more. 1 dc in each of next 16 (**17**-20) ch. Turn.

2nd row: Ch 3 (counts as 1 dc). Miss first dc. 1 dc in each of next 15 (**16**-19) dc. *Miss next ch-2 sp. 5 dc in next dc. Ch 2. Miss next 4 dc.* 1 dc in each of next 5 dc. Rep from * to * once more. 1 dc in each of next 16 (**17**-20) dc. Turn.**

Rep 2nd row until work from beg measures 12 (**12½**-12½) ins [30.5 (**34.5**-34.5) cm] ending with WS facing for next row.

***Shape Armhole: 1st row: Sl st in each of first 10 dc. Ch 3. Miss last dc where last sl st was worked. 1 dc in each of next 6 (**7**-10) dc. *Miss next ch-2 sp. 5 dc in next dc. Ch 2. Miss next 4 dc.* 1 dc in each of next 5 dc. Rep from * to * once more. 1 dc in each of next 16 (**17**-20) dc. Turn.

2nd row: Ch 3. Miss first dc. 1 dc in each of next 15 (**16**-19) dc. *Miss next ch-2 sp. 5 dc in next dc. Ch 2. Miss next 4 dc.* 1 dc in each of

next 5 dc. Rep from * to * once more. 1 dc in each of next 7 (**8**-11) dc. Turn.

3rd row: Ch 3. Miss first dc. 1 dc in each of next 6 (**7**-10) dc. *Miss next ch-2 sp. 5 dc in next dc. Ch 2. Miss next 4 dc.* 1 dc in each of next 5 dc. Rep from * to * once more. 1 dc in each of next 16 (**17**-20) dc. Turn.***

Rep 2nd and 3rd rows until work from beg measures 15 (**15½**-16) ins [38 (**39.5**-40.5) cm], ending with RS facing for next row.

****Shape Neck: 1st row: Sl st in each of first 6 dc. Ch 3. Miss last dc where last sl st was worked. *(Yoh. Draw up a loop in next st. Yoh and draw through 2 loops on hook) twice. Yoh and draw through all loops on hook* – dc2tog made. 1 dc in each of next 8 (**9**-12) dc. *Miss next ch-2 sp. 5 dc in next dc. Ch 2. Miss next 4 dc.* 1 dc in each of next 5 dc. Rep from * to * once more. 1 dc in each of next 7 (**8**-11) dc. Turn.

2nd row: Ch 3. Miss first dc. 1 dc in each of next 6 (**7**-10) dc. *Miss next ch-2 sp. 5 dc in next dc. Ch 2. Miss next 4 dc.* 1 dc in each of next 5 dc. Rep from * to * once more. 1 dc in each of next 8 (**9**-12) dc. Dc2tog over last 2 sts. Turn.

3rd row: Ch 3. Miss first st. Dc2tog over next 2 dc. 1 dc in each of next 6 (**7**-10) dc. *Miss next ch-2 sp. 5 dc in next dc. Ch 2. Miss next 4 dc.* 1 dc in each of next 5 dc. Rep from * to * once more. 1 dc in each of next 7 (8-11) dc. Turn.

4th row: Ch 3. Miss first dc. 1 dc in each of next 6 (7-10) dc. *Miss next ch-2 sp. 5 dc in next dc. Ch 2. Miss next 4 dc.* 1 dc in each of next 5 dc. Rep from * to * once more. 1 dc in each of next 6 (7-10) dc. Dc2tog over last 2 sts. Turn.

5th row: Ch 3. Miss first st. Dc2tog over next 2 dc. 1 dc in each of next 4 (4-7) dc. *Miss next ch 2 sp. 5 dc in next dc. Ch 2. Miss next 4 dc.* 1 dc in each of next 5 dc. Rep from * to * once more. 1 dc in each of next 7 (8-11) dc. Turn.

6th row: Ch 3. Miss first dc. 1 dc in each of next 6 (7-10) dc. *Miss next ch-2 sp. 5 dc in next dc. Ch 2. Miss next 4 dc.* 1 dc in each of next 5 dc. Rep from * to * once more. 1 dc in each of next 4 (4-7) dc. Dc2tog over last 2 sts. Turn.

7th row: Ch 3. Miss first st. Dc2tog over next 2 dc. 1 dc in each of next 1 (2-5) dc. *Miss next ch-2 sp. 5 dc in next dc. Ch 2. Miss next 4 dc.* 1 dc in each of next 5 dc. Rep from * to * once more. 1 dc in each of next 7 (8-11) dc. Turn.

8th row: Ch 3. Miss first dc. 1 dc in each of next 6 (7-10) dc. *Miss next ch-2 sp. 5 dc in next dc. Ch 2. Miss next 4 dc.* 1 dc in each of next 5 dc. Rep from * to * once more. 1 dc in each of next 1 (2-5) dc. Dc2tog over last 2 sts. Turn.

9th row: Ch 3. Miss first st. (Dc2tog over next 2 sts) 0 (1-1) time. 1 dc in each of next 1 (0-3) dc. *Miss next ch-2 sp. 5 dc in next dc. Ch 2. Miss next 4 dc.* 1 dc in each of next 5 dc. Rep from * to * once more. 1 dc in each of next 7 (8-11) dc. Turn.

10th row: Ch 3. Miss first dc. 1 dc in each of next 6 (7-10) dc. *Miss next ch-2 sp. 5 dc in next dc. Ch 2. Miss next 4 dc.* 1 dc in each of next 5 dc. Rep from * to * once more. 1 dc in each of next 2 (2-3) dc. (Dc2tog over last 2 sts) 0 (0-1) time. Turn.

11th row: Ch 3. Miss first st. 1 dc in each of next 1 (1-3) dc. *Miss next ch-2 sp. 5 dc in next dc. Ch 2. Miss next 4 dc.* 1 dc in each of next 5 dc. Rep from * to * once more. 1 dc in each of next 7 (8-11) dc. Turn.

12th row: Ch 3. Miss first dc. 1 dc in each of next 6 (7-10) dc. *Miss next ch-2 sp. 5 dc in next dc. Ch 2. Miss next 4 dc.* 1 dc in each of next 5 dc. Rep from * to * once more. 1 dc in each of last 2 (2-4) sts. Fasten off.

Lower Edging: With RS of work facing join yarn with sl st to first st of opposite side of foundation ch. Ch 3. Work 50 (50-56) dc across opposite side of foundation ch. Turn.

INSTRUCTIONS CONT.

1st row: Ch 3 (counts as 1 dc). Miss first dc. *1 dc in next dc. Miss next 2 dc. 5 dc in next dc. Ch 2. Miss next 2 dc. Rep from * to last 2 dc. 1 dc in each of last 2 dc. Turn.

2nd row: Ch 3. Miss first dc. *1 dc in next dc. Miss next ch-2 sp. 5 dc in next dc. Ch 2. Miss next 4 dc. Rep from * ending with 1 dc in each of last 2 dc. Fasten off.****

LEFT FRONT

Work from ** to ** as given for Right Front.

Rep 2nd row until work from beg measures 12 (12½-12½) ins [30.5 (34.5-34.5) cm] ending with RS facing for next row.

Work from *** to *** as given for Right Front.

Rep 2nd and 3rd rows until work from beg measures 15 (15½-16) ins [38 (39.5-40.5) cm] ending with WS facing for next row.

Work from **** to **** as given for Right Front.

BACK

Ch 100 (106-116).

1st row: (RS). 1 dc in 4th ch from hook. 1 dc in each of next 14 (15-18) ch. *Miss next 2 ch. 5 dc in next ch. Ch 2. Miss next 3 ch.* 1 dc in each of next 5 ch. Rep from * to * once more. 1 dc in each of next 32 (36-40) ch. Rep from * to * once more.

1 dc in each of next 5 ch. Rep from * to * once more. 1 dc in each of next 16 (17-20) ch. Turn.

2nd row: Ch 3. Miss first dc. 1 dc in each of next 14 (15-18) dc. *Miss next ch-2 sp. 5 dc in next dc. Ch 2. Miss next 4 dc.* 1 dc in each of next 5 dc. Rep from * to * once more. 1 dc in each of next 32 (36-40) dc. Rep from * to * once more. 1 dc in each of next 5 dc. Rep from * to * once more. 1 dc in each of next 16 (17-20) dc. Turn.

Rep 2nd row until work from beg measures 12 (12½-12½) ins [30.5 (34.5-34.5) cm] ending with RS facing for next row.

Shape Armholes: Next row: Sl st in each of first 10 dc. Ch 3. Miss last dc where last sl st was made. Work in pat to last 9 dc. Turn. Leave rem sts unworked.

Cont even in pat until work from beg measures same length as Fronts to shoulder, ending with RS facing for next row. Fasten off.

Lower Edging: With RS of work facing join yarn with sl st to first st of opposite side of foundation ch. Ch 3. Work 98 (104-116) dc across opposite side of foundation ch. Turn.

1st row: Ch 3 (counts as 1 dc). Miss first dc. *1 dc in next dc. Miss next 2 dc. 5 dc in next dc. Ch 2. Miss next 2 dc. Rep from * to last 2 dc. 1 dc in each of last 2 dc. Turn.

2nd row: Ch 3. Miss first dc. *1 dc in next dc. Miss next ch-2 sp. 5 dc in next dc. Ch 2. Miss next 4 dc. Rep from * ending with 1 dc in each of last 2 dc. Fasten off.

SLEEVES

Ch 59 (59-63).

1st row: (RS). 1 dc in 4th ch from hook. 1 dc in each of next 18 (18-20) ch. *Miss next 2 ch. 5 dc in next ch. Ch 2. Miss next 3 ch.* 1 dc in each of next 5 ch. Rep from * to * once more. 1 dc in each of next 20 (20-22) ch. Turn.

2nd row: Ch 3. Miss first dc. 1 dc in each of next 19 (19-21) dc. *Miss next ch-2 sp. 5 dc in next dc. Ch 2. Miss next 4 dc.* 1 dc in each of next 5 dc. Rep from * to * once more. 1 dc in each of next 20 (20-22) dc. Turn.

3rd row: (Increase row). Ch 3. 1 dc in first dc (inc made). 1 dc in each of next 19 (19-21) dc. *Miss next ch-2 sp. 5 dc in next dc. Ch 2. Miss next 4 dc.* 1 dc in each of next 5 dc. Rep from * to * once more. 1 dc in each of next 19 (19-21) dc. 2 dc in last dc (inc made). Turn.

Cont in pat, inc 1 st each end of following 4th rows until the row "**Ch 3. Miss first dc. 1 dc in each of next 26 (26-28) dc. *Miss next ch 2-sp. 5 dc in next dc. Ch 2. Miss next 4 dc.* 1 dc in each of next 5 dc. Rep from * to * once more.**

1 dc in each of next 27 (27-29) dc. Turn." - has been worked.

Cont even in pat until Sleeve measures 9½ (10½-11½) ins [24 (26.5-29) cm], ending with RS facing for next row.

Shape Top: 1st row: Sl st in each of first 7 dc. Ch 3. Miss last dc where last sl st was worked. *(Yoh. Draw up a loop in next st. Yoh and draw through 2 loops on hook) 3 times. Yoh and draw through all loops on hook – dc3tog made.* 1 dc in each of next 17 (17-19) dc. *Miss next ch-2 sp. 5 dc in next dc. Ch 2. Miss next 4 dc.* 1 dc in each of next 5 dc. Rep from * to * once more. 1 dc in each of next 18 (18-20) dc. Dc3tog over last 3 dc. **Turn.** Leave rem sts unworked.

2nd row: Ch 3. Miss first st. Dc3tog over next 3 dc. 1 dc in each of next 15 (15-17) dc. *Miss next ch-2 sp. 5 dc in next dc. Ch 2. Miss next 4 dc.* 1 dc in each of next 5 dc. Rep from * to * once more. 1 dc in each of next 16 (16-17) dc. Dc3tog over last 3 sts. Turn.

3rd row: Ch 3. Miss first dc. Dc3tog over next 3 dc. 1 dc in each of next 13 (13-15) sts. *Miss next ch-2 sp. 5 dc in next dc. Ch 2. Miss next 4 dc.* 1 dc in each of next 5 dc. Rep from * to * once more. 1 dc in each of next 14 (14-16) dc. Dc3tog over last 3 dc. Turn.

INSTRUCTIONS CONT.

4th row: Ch 3. Miss first dc. Dc3tog over next 3 dc. 1 dc in each of next 11 (**11**-13) dc. *Miss next ch-2 sp. 5 dc in next dc. Ch 2. Miss next 4 dc.* 1 dc in each of next 5 dc. Rep from * to * once more. 1 dc in each of next 12 (**12**-14) dc. Dc3tog over last 3 dc. Turn.

5th row: Ch 3. Miss first dc. Dc3tog over next 3 dc. 1 dc in each of next 9 (**9**-11) dc. *Miss next ch-2 sp. 5 dc in next dc. Ch 2. Miss next 4 dc.* 1 dc in each of next 5 dc. Rep from * to * once more. 1 dc in each of next 10 (**10**-12) dc. Dc3tog over last 3 dc. Fasten off.

Lower Edging: With RS of work facing join yarn with sl st to first st of opposite side of foundation ch. Ch 3. Work 57 (**57**-61) dc across opposite side of foundation ch. Turn.

1st row: Ch 3 (counts as 1 dc). Miss first dc. 1 dc in each of next 1 (**1**-0) dc. *1 dc in next dc. Miss next 2 dc. 5 dc in next dc. Ch 2. Miss next 2 dc. Rep from * to last 2 (**2**-1) dc. 1 dc in each of last 2 (**2**-1) dc. Turn.

2nd row: Ch 3. Miss first dc. 1 dc in each of next 1 (**1**-2) dc. *Miss next ch-2 sp. 5 dc in next dc. Ch 2. Miss next 4 dc. 1 dc in next dc. Rep from * ending with 1 dc in last dc. Fasten off.

FINISHING

Pin garment pieces to measurements. Steam lightly and cover with a damp cloth leaving to dry.

Sew shoulder seams.

Front and Neck Edging: With RS of work facing join yarn with sl st to first st at bottom corner of Right Front. Ch 1. 1 sc in same sp. Work 1 row sc evenly up Right Front to neck shaping. 3 sc in corner. Work 1 row sc evenly around right neck edge to opposite corner. 3 sc in corner. Work 1 row sc evenly down Left Front edge. Turn.

Next row: Ch 1. 1 sc in each sc to Left Front neck edge corner. 3 sc in corner st. 1 sc in each sc around neck edge to opposite corner. Ch 6 for button loop. 1 sc in same sp as last sc. 1 sc in each sc down Right Front. Fasten off.

Sew in sleeves. Sew side and sleeve seams. Sew on button.

Crochet Button: (Optional) With smaller crochet hook, ch 2, leaving an end 6 ins [15 cm] long.

1st rnd: Work 6 sc in 2nd ch from hook. Join with sl st to first sc.

2nd rnd: Ch 1. Work 2 sc in each sc around. Join with sl st to first sc.

3rd rnd: Push end into center of button for stuffing. Ch 1. *Draw up a loop in each of next 2 sc. Yoh and draw through 3 loops on hook – sc2tog made.* (Sc2tog) 5 times more. Join with sl st to first sc.

4th rnd: Ch 1. (Sc2tog) 3 times. Join with sl st to first sc. Fasten off and thread end through tapestry needle and draw around final sts of last round tightly. Sew on button to correspond to button loop.

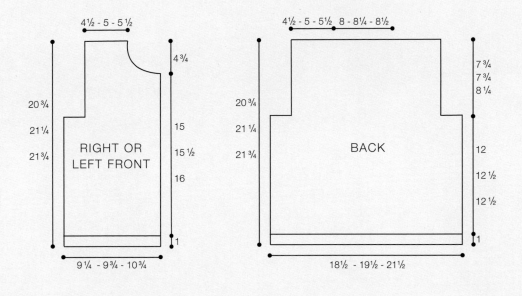

RIGHT OR LEFT FRONT

4½ - 5 - 5½

4¾

20¾
21¼
21¾

15
15½
16

1

9¼ - 9¾ - 10¾

BACK

4½ - 5 - 5½   8 - 8¼ - 8½

7¾
7¾
8¼

20¾
21¼
21¾

12
12½
12½

1

18½ - 19½ - 21½

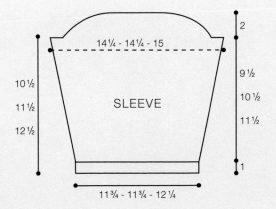

SLEEVE

2

14¼ - 14¼ - 15

9½
10½
11½

10½
11½
12½

1

11¾ - 11¾ - 12¼

Nautical Top

SIZES

Bust measurement

Extra-Small	32 ins	[81.5	cm]
Small	34 "	[86.5	"]
Medium	36 "	[91.5	"]
Large	38 "	[96.5	"]
Extra-Large	40 "	[101.5	"]

Finished bust

Extra-Small	34 ins	[86.5	cm]
Small	36 "	[91.5	"]
Medium	38 "	[96.5	"]
Large	40 "	[101.5	"]
Extra-Large	42 "	[106.5	"]

MATERIALS

Patons Grace (50 g/1.75 oz)

Sizes	XS	S	M	L	XL	
Main Color (MC) (60104 Azure)						
	2	2	2	3	3	balls
Contrast A (60130 Sky)						
	3	3	3	4	4	balls
Contrast B (60005 Snow)						
	4	5	5	5	6	balls

Size 4.00 mm (U.S. G or 6) crochet hook **or size needed to obtain tension.**

TENSION

24 sts and 23 rows = 4 ins [10 cm] in pat.

INSTRUCTIONS

The instructions are written for smallest size. If changes are necessary for larger sizes the instructions will be written thus ( ).

STRIPE PAT

With MC, work 8 rows.

With A, work 2 rows.

With MC, work 6 rows.

With A, work 2 rows.

With MC, work 4 rows.

With A, work 2 rows.

With MC, work 2 rows.

With A, work 4 rows.

With MC, work 2 rows.

With A, work 6 rows.

With MC, work 2 rows.

With A, work 8 rows.

With B, work 2 rows.

With A, work 6 rows.

With B, work 2 rows.

With A, work 4 rows.

With B, work 2 rows.

With A, work 2 rows.

With B, work 4 rows.

With A, work 2 rows.

With B, work 6 rows.

With A, work 2 rows.

With B, work 8 rows.

With A, work 2 rows.

With B, work 8 rows.

With A, work 2 rows.

These 100 rows form Stripe Pat.

FRONT

With MC, ch 104 (110**-116-**122**-128).

Foundation row: (RS). 1 sc in 2nd ch from hook. *Ch 1. Miss next ch. 1 sc in next ch. Rep from * to end of ch. Turn. 103 (**109**-115-**121**-127) sts.

1st row: Ch 1. 1 sc in first sc. *1 sc in next ch-1 sp. Ch 1. Miss next sc. Rep from * to last 2 sts. 1 sc in next ch-1 sp. 1 sc in last sc. Turn. (First row of Stripe Pat is complete)

2nd row: Ch 1. 1 sc in first sc. *Ch 1. Miss next sc. 1 sc in next ch-1 sp. Rep from * to last sc. 1 sc in last sc. Turn.

Last 2 rows form pat.

First 2 rows of Stripe Pat are completed.

Cont in pat, keeping cont of Stripe Pat until work from beg measures 2 ins [5 cm]. Place first set of markers at each end of last row.

Cont in Stripe Pat until work from beg measures 15 (**15**-16-**16**-16½) ins [38 (**38**-40.5-**40.5**-42) cm], ending with RS facing for next row.

Note: When 100 rows of Stripe Pat are complete, cont in pat with B only.

Armhole shaping: 1st row: Sl st in each of first 5 sts. Ch 1. Pat to last 5 sts. **Turn.** Leave rem sts unworked. 93 (**99**-105-**111**-117) sts.

2nd row: Work even in pat.

3rd row: Ch 1. *Draw up a loop in each of first 2 sts. Yoh and draw through all 3 loops on hook – Sc2tog made. Pat to last 2 sts. Sc2tog over last 2 sts. Turn.**

Rep last 2 rows 3 times more. 85 (**91**-97-**103**-109) sts.

V-neck shaping: Next row: (RS). Ch 1. Sc2tog over first 2 sts. Pat across next 38 (**41**-44-**47**-50) sts. Sc2tog over next 2 sts. **Turn.** Leave rem sts unworked. 40 (**43**-46-**49**-52) sts.

Next row: Ch 1. Sc2tog over first 2 sts. Pat to end of row. Turn.

Next row: Ch 1. Sc2tog over first 2 sts. Pat to last 2 sts. Sc2tog over last 2 sts. Turn.

Next row: Ch 1. Sc2tog over first 2 sts. Pat to end of row. Turn.

Rep last 2 rows 4 (**5**-3-**1**-1) time(s) more. 24 (**24**-33-**42**-39) sts.

Sizes S, M ,L and XL only: Next row: (RS). Ch 1. Pat to last 2 sts. Sc2tog over last 2 sts. Turn.

Next row: Ch 1. Pat to end of row. Turn.

Rep last 2 rows (**1**-3-**5**-3) time(s) more. (**20**-25-**30**-31) sts.

All Sizes: Next row: (RS). Ch 1. Pat to last 2 sts. Sc2tog over last 2 sts. Turn.

Next row: Work even in pat. Turn.

Rep last 2 rows 8 (**3**-7-**9**-9) times more. 15 (**16**-17-**20**-21) sts.

Size S only: With B, work 6 rows even in pat.

All Sizes: Fasten off.

With RS of work facing, miss next st. Join appropriate color with sl st to next st. Ch 1. Sc2tog over first 2 sts. Pat to last 2 sts. Sc2tog over last 2 sts. Turn. 40 (**43**-46-**49**-52) sts.

Next row: Ch 1. Pat to last 2 sts. Sc2tog over last 2 sts. Turn.

Next row: Ch 1. Sc2tog over first 2 sts. Pat to last 2 sts. Sc2tog over last 2 sts. Turn.

Next row: Ch 1. Pat to last 2 sts. Sc2tog over last 2 sts. Turn.

Rep last 2 rows 4 (**5**-3-**1**-1) time(s) more. 24 (**24**-33-**42**-39) sts.

Sizes S, M, L and XL only: Next row: (RS). Ch 1. Sc2tog over first 2 sts. Pat to end of row. Turn.

Next row: Ch 1. Pat to end of row. Turn.

Rep last 2 rows (**1**-3-**5**-3) time(s) more. (**20**-25-**30**-31) sts.

INSTRUCTIONS CONT.

All Sizes: Next row: (RS). Ch 1. Sc2tog over first 2 sts. Pat to end of row. Turn.

Next row: Work even in pat. Turn.

Rep last 2 rows 8 (3-7-9-9) times more. 15 (16-17-20-21) sts.

Size S only: With B, work 6 rows even in pat.

All Sizes: Fasten off.

BACK

Work from ** to ** as given for Front.

Rep last 2 rows 9 (12-12-12-12) times more. 73 (73-79-85-91) sts.

With B, cont even in pat until armhole measures same length as Front to shoulders, ending with RS facing for next row. Fasten off.

FINISHING

Sew shoulder seams. Place second set of markers ¼ inch [5 mm] up along left and right sides of V-neck shaping from V.

COLLAR: With RS of work facing, join B at marked st of right side of V-neck shaping with sl st. Ch 1. 1 sc in same sp as last sl st. Work 30 (32-34-38-38) sc up right side of V-neck shaping. Pat across 43 (45-45-45-49) sts across back

neck edge. Work 31 (33-35-39-39) sc down left side of V-neck shaping to marked st. Turn.

Proceed in pat as given for Front until Collar from beg measures 3 ins [7.5 cm], ending with RS facing for next row. Fasten off.

Collar Edging: With RS of Collar facing, join B with sl st at 1st row of Collar. Ch 1. 1 sc in same sp as last sl st. 13 sc up left side of Collar. 3 sc in corner. 93 (98-102-110-112) sc across long edge of Collar. 3 sc in corner. 13 sc down right side of Collar. Join A. Turn.

Next row: With A, working in back loops only, 1 sc in each sc to end of row, working 3 sc in corners. Join B. Turn.

Next row: With B, as 2nd row. Fasten off.

Sew sides of Collar Edging to V-neck edge. Sew side seams above first set of markers.

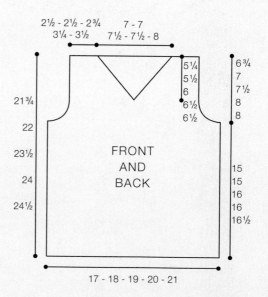

2½ - 2½ - 2¾   7 - 7
3¼ - 3½   7½ - 7½ - 8

5¼
5½
6
6½
6½

6¾
7
7½
8
8

21¾

22

23½

24

24½

FRONT
AND
BACK

15
15
16
16
16½

17 - 18 - 19 - 20 - 21

Daisy Mesh Vest

SIZES

To fit bust measurement

Extra-Small	32	ins	[81.5	cm]
Small/Med	34-36	"	[86.5- 91.5	"]
Large	38	"	[96.5	"]
Extra-Large	40-42	"	[101.5-106.5	"]

Finished bust

Extra-Small	35¾	ins	[91	cm]
Small/Med	39	"	[99	"]
Large	42	"	[106.5	"]
Extra-Large	45	"	[114.5	"]

MATERIALS

Patons Grace (50 g/1.75 oz)

Sizes	XS	S/M	L	XL	
Vest					
60008 Natural	**6**	**7**	**7**	**8**	**balls**

Sizes 3.00 mm (U.S. C or 2) and 3.50 mm (U.S. E or 4) crochet hooks **or size needed to obtain tension**.

TENSION

26 sts and 9 rows = 4 ins [10 cm] in Flower Pat with larger hook.

INSTRUCTIONS

The instructions are written for smallest size. If changes are necessary for larger sizes the instructions will be written thus ( ).

Note: Body is worked in one piece to armholes.

BODY

With larger hook, ch 235 (**255**-275-**295**).

Foundation row: (RS). 1 dc in 5th ch from hook (turning ch counts as 1 dc and ch-1 sp). *Ch 1. Miss next ch. 1 dc in next ch. Rep from * to end of ch. Turn. 233 (**253**-273-**293**) sts.

***1st row: Ch 4 (counts as 1 dc and ch-1 sp). *1 dc in next dc. Ch 1. Miss next ch-1 sp. Rep from *, ending with 1 dc in last dc. Turn.

2nd row: Ch 4 (counts as 1 dc and ch-1 sp). 1 dc in next dc. *Ch 3. *(Yoh and draw up a loop. Yoh and draw through 2 loops on hook) twice into top of last dc worked. (Yoh and draw up a loop. Yoh and draw through 2 loops on hook) 3 times in next dc of previous row. Miss next dc. (Yoh and draw up a loop. Yoh and draw through 2 loops on hook) 3 times in next dc. Yoh and draw through all 9 loops on hook. Ch 1 – double cluster made. Ch 3. (Yoh and draw up a loop. Yoh and draw through 2 loops on hook) twice into top of double cluster. Yoh and draw through 3 loops on hook – Bottom 4 Petals made.** (see Diagram on pg. 157).* (1 dc in next dc. Ch 1. Miss next ch-1 sp) 6 times. 1 dc in next dc. Rep from * to last 10 sts. Rep from * to ** once more. 1 dc in next dc. Ch 1. Miss next ch-1 sp. 1 dc in last dc. Turn.

3rd row: Ch 4 (counts as 1 dc and ch-1 sp). *1 dc in next dc. Ch 1. [*(Yoh and draw up a loop. Yoh and draw through 2 loops on hook) 3 times. Yoh and draw through all loops on hook-dc3tog cluster made. Ch 3. Dc3tog cluster]* all in top of *Bottom 4 Petals*-Top 2 Petals made (see Diagram on pg. 157). Ch 1.** (1 dc in next dc. Ch 1. Miss next ch-1 sp) 6 times. Rep from * to last flower. Rep from * to ** once more. 1 dc in next dc. Ch 1. Miss next ch-1 sp. 1 dc in last dc. Turn.

4th row: Ch 4 (counts as 1 dc and ch-1 sp). 1 dc in next dc. *Ch 1. Miss next ch-1 sp. 1 dc in next dc3tog. Ch 1. Miss next ch. 1 dc in next ch. Ch 1. Miss next ch. 1 dc in next dc3tog.** (Ch 1. Miss next ch-1 sp. 1 dc in next dc) 7 times. Rep from * to last flower. Rep from * to ** once more. (Ch 1. Miss next ch-1 sp. 1 dc in next dc) twice. Turn.

5th to 7th rows: As 1st row.

8th row: Ch 4 (counts as 1 dc and ch-1 sp). (1 dc in next dc. Ch 1. Miss next ch-1 sp) 5 times. *1 dc in next dc. Bottom 4 Petals over next 7 sts. (1 dc in next dc. Ch 1. Miss next ch-1 sp) 6 times. Rep from * to last st. 1 dc in last dc. Turn.

9th row: Ch 4 (counts as 1 dc and ch-1 sp). (1 dc in next dc. Ch 1. Miss next ch-1 sp) 5 times. *1 dc in next dc. Ch 1. Top 2 Petals in next Bottom 4 Petals. Ch 1. (1 dc in next dc. Ch 1. Miss next ch-1 sp) 6 times. Rep from * to last st. 1 dc in last dc. Turn.

10th row: Ch 4 (counts as 1 dc and ch-1 sp). (1 dc in next dc. Ch 1. Miss next ch-1 sp) 6 times. *1 dc in next dc3tog. Ch 1. Miss next ch. 1 dc in next ch. Ch 1. Miss next ch. 1 dc in next dc3tog. (Ch 1. Miss next ch-1 sp. 1 dc in next dc) 7 times. Ch 1. Miss next ch-1 sp. Rep from * to last st. 1 dc in last st. Turn.

11th to 13th rows: As 1st row.

Rows 2 to 13 form Flower Pat.***

Work a further 22 rows in Flower Pat, thus ending on a 11th row of pat.

Divide for Armholes: Next row: (RS). Pat across next 43 (49-49-53) sts for Right Front. **Turn.** Leave rem sts unworked.

Cont on last 43 (49-49-53) sts for Right Front.

Keeping cont of Flower Pat, proceed as follows:

**Next row: Ch 3 (counts as dc). Miss next ch-1 sp. 1 dc in next dc. Pat to last 3 sts. 1 dc in next dc. Miss next ch-1 sp. 1 dc in last dc. Turn.

Next row: Ch 3 (counts as dc). 1 dc in next dc. Miss next ch-1 sp. 1 dc in next dc. Pat to last 4 sts. 1 dc in next dc. Ch 1. Miss next ch-1 sp and next dc. 1 dc in top of ch 3. Turn.

Next row: Ch 3 (counts as dc). Miss next ch-1 sp. 1 dc in next dc. Pat to last 3 sts. 1 dc in next dc. Miss next dc. 1 dc in top of ch 3. Turn.**

Rep last 2 rows 2 (4-5-5) times more. 29 (27-23-27) sts.

Next row: (RS). Ch 3 (counts as dc). 1 dc in next dc. Miss next ch-1 sp. 1 dc in next dc. Pat to last 4 sts. 1 dc in next dc. Ch 1. Miss next ch-1 sp and next dc. 1 dc in top of ch 3. Turn.

Next row: Pat to last 3 sts. 1 dc in next dc. Miss next dc. 1 dc in top of ch 3. Turn.

Sizes XS, S/M and XL only: Next row: (RS). Ch 3 (counts as dc). 1 dc in next dc. Miss next ch-1 sp. 1 dc in next dc. Pat to end of row. Turn.

Rep last 2 rows 2 (1-1) time(s) more. 21 sts.

Next row: Pat to last 3 sts. 1 dc in next dc. Ch 1. Miss next dc. 1 dc in top of ch 3. Turn.

All Sizes: Work 3 (0-3-0) rows even in pat. Fasten off.

Back: With RS of work facing, miss next 25 (25-33-37) sts. Join yarn with sl st to next st. Ch 4 (counts as 1 dc and ch-1 sp). (1 dc in next dc. Ch 1. Miss next ch-1 sp) 47 (51-53-55) times. 1 dc in next dc. **Turn.** Leave rem sts unworked.

Work from ** to ** as given for Right Front.

INSTRUCTIONS CONT.

Rep last 2 rows 3 (4-6-6) times more. 81 (85-81-85) sts.

Cont even in pat until armhole measures same length as Right Front. Fasten off.

Left Front: With RS of work facing, miss next 25 (25-33-37) sts. Join yarn with sl st to next st. Ch 4 (counts as 1 dc and ch-1 sp). Pat to end of row. Turn. Work from ** to ** as given for Right Front. Rep last 2 rows 2 (4-5-5) times more. 29 (27-23-27) sts.

Next row: (RS). Ch 4 (counts as 1 dc and ch-1). Miss next dc and ch-1 sp. 1 dc in next dc. Pat to last 4 sts. 1 dc in next dc. Ch 1. Miss next ch-1 sp and next dc. 1 dc in top of ch 3. Turn.

Next row: Ch 3 (counts as dc). Miss next ch-1 sp. 1 dc in next dc. Pat to end of row. Turn.

Sizes XS, S/M and XL only: Next row: Pat to last 4 sts. 1 dc in next dc. Ch 1. Miss next ch-1 sp and next dc. 1 dc in top of ch 3. Turn.

Rep last 2 rows 2 (1-1) time(s) more. 21 sts.

Next row: Ch 3 (counts as dc). Miss next ch-1 sp. 1 dc in next dc. Pat to end of row. Turn.

All Sizes: Work 3 (0-3-0) rows even in pat. Fasten off.

FINISHING

Sew shoulder seams.

Armhole Edging: With RS of work facing and smaller hook, join yarn with sl st at shoulder. Ch 1. Work 90 (96-96-102) sc evenly around armhole edge. Join with sl st to first sc.

Next rnd: Ch 1. 1 sc in each sc around. Join with sl st to first sc.

Next rnd: Ch 1. 1 sc in first sc. *Ch 3. Miss next 2 sc. (Yoh and draw up a loop. Yoh and draw through 2 loops on hook) 3 times in next sc. Yoh and draw through all loops on hook - dc3tog cluster made. Ch 3. Miss next 2 sc. 1 sc in next sc. Rep from * around ending with: join with sl st in first sc. Fasten off.

Bottom Edging: With RS of work facing and smaller hook, join yarn with sl st at corner of Left Front. Ch 1. Work 1 row of sc evenly across lower edge. Ch 1. **Do not** turn.

Next row: Working from left to right instead of from right to left, as usual, work 1 reverse sc in each sc across. Fasten off.

Neck Edging: With RS of work facing and smaller hook. join yarn with sl st at corner of Bottom Edging on Right Front. Ch 1. Work 111 (114-120-120) sc evenly up Right Front edge, 31 (37-37-43) sc across back neck edge and 111 (114-120-120) sc down Left Front edge. 253 (265-277-283) sc. Turn.

Place markers for 5 buttonholes on Right Front edge having bottom buttonhole 1 inch [2.5 cm] above lower edge, top buttonhole at beg of V-neck shaping and rem 3 buttonholes spaced evenly between.

Next row: Ch 1. 1 sc in each sc across. Turn.

Next row: Ch 1. 1 sc in each sc across to first buttonhole marker. *Ch 2. Miss next 2 sc. 1 sc in each sc to next buttonhole marker. Rep from * 3 times more. Ch 2. Miss next 2 sc. 1 sc in each sc to end of row. Turn.

Next row: Ch 1. *1 sc in each sc to next ch-2 sp. 2 sc in next ch-2 sp. Rep from * 4 times more. 1 sc in each sc to end of row. Turn.

Next row: Ch 1. 1 sc in first sc. *Ch 3. Miss next 2 sc. Dc3tog cluster in next sc. Ch 3. Miss next 2 sc. 1 sc in next sc. Rep from * to end of row. Fasten off.

BUTTONS: (Make 5).

With smaller hook, ch 2, leaving an end approx 5 ins [12.5 cm] long at beg of chain.

1st rnd: 6 sc in 2nd ch from hook. Join with sl st in first sc.

2nd rnd: Ch 1. 2 sc in each sc around. Join with sl st in first sc.

3rd rnd: Ch 1. *Draw up a loop in each of next 2 sc. Yoh and draw through all loops on hook – sc2tog made. Rep from * around. Join with sl st to first st. Fasten off, leaving an end approx 5 ins [12.5 cm] long.

Thread end through tapestry needle. Stuff end at beg of chain into button.

Thread end on needle through rem 6 sts and draw up tightly. Sew in position to Left Front to correspond to buttonhole.

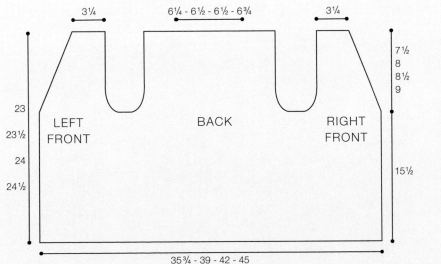

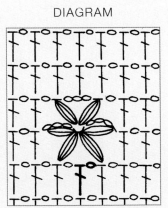

DIAGRAM

Pretty V Neck

SIZES

Bust measurement

Extra-Small/Small	32-34	ins	[81.5-86.5	cm]
Medium/Large	36-38	"	[91.5-96.5	"]
Extra-Large	40	"	[101.5	"]

Finished bust

Extra-Small/Small	36	ins	[91.5	cm]
Medium/Large	40	"	[101.5	"]
Extra-Large	44	"	[112	"]

MATERIALS

Patons Grace (50 g/1.75 oz)

Sizes	XS/S	M/L	XL	
60008 (Natural)	**9**	**10**	**11**	**balls**

Sizes 3.25 mm (U.S. D or 3) and 3.50 mm (U.S. E or 4) crochet hooks **or size needed to obtain tension**.

TENSION

4 Shells and 13 rows = 4 ins [10 cm] in pat with smaller hook.

INSTRUCTIONS

The instructions are written for smallest size. If changes are necessary for larger sizes the instructions will be written thus ( ).

FRONT

** With larger hook, ch 110 (122-134).

Foundation row: (RS). 1 sc in 2nd ch from hook. *Miss next 2 ch. [*(1 dc. Ch 2) twice. 1 dc*] all in next ch* - Shell made. Miss next 2 ch. 1 sc in next ch. Rep from * to end of ch. 18 (**20**-22) Shells.

1st row: Ch 5 (counts as dc and ch 2). 1 dc in first sc. *Miss next dc and ch-2 sp. 1 sc in next dc (top of Shell). Miss next ch-2 sp and dc. Shell in next sc. Rep from * to last Shell. Miss next dc and ch-2 sp. 1 sc in next dc (top of Shell). (1 dc. Ch 2. 1 dc) all in last sc. Turn.

2nd row: Ch 1. 1 sc in first dc. *Shell in next sc. Miss next dc and ch-2 sp. 1 sc in top of Shell. Miss next dc and ch-2 sp. Rep from * to last sc. Shell in next sc. 1 sc in 3rd ch of turning ch 5. Turn.

Last 2 rows form pat.

Cont in pat until work from beg measures 16 (**16½**-17) ins [40 (**42**-43) cm], ending with RS facing for next row.

Armhole shaping: 1st row: Sl st in [first dc, ch-2 sp, dc, sc, (dc, ch-2 sp) twice, dc, sc, dc, ch-2 sp and dc]. Ch 1. 1 sc in same sp as last sl st. Pat to last 2 shells. Miss next dc, and ch-2 sp. 1 sc in next dc. **Turn.** Leave rem sts unworked. 14 (**16**-18) Shells.

2nd row: Sl st in [first sc, dc, ch-2 sp and dc]. Ch 1. 1 sc in same sp as last sl st. Pat to last Shell. Miss next dc and ch-2 sp. 1 sc in next dc. **Turn.** Leave rem sts unworked.

Rep last row 1 (**1**-2) time(s) more. 12 (**14**-14) Shells.**

Sizes XS/S and M/L only: Work 1 row even in pat.

All Sizes: V-neck shaping: 1st row: (RS). Pat across 6 (**7**-7) Shells, ending with 1 sc in top of last shell. **Turn.** Leave rem sts unworked.

2nd row: Ch 3 (counts as dc). 1 dc in first sc. 1 sc in top of next Shell. Pat to end of row. Turn.

3rd row: Pat across, ending with 1 sc in top of last Shell. (1 dc. Ch 2. 1 dc) in next sc. 1 dc in top of turning ch 3. Turn.

4th row: Ch 3. Miss first 2 dc. 1 dc in next ch-2 sp. Miss next dc. Shell in next sc. Pat to end of row. Turn.

5th row: Pat across, ending with 1 sc in top of last Shell. 1 dc in top of turning ch 3. Turn.

6th row: Ch 3. Miss first dc. (1 dc. Ch 2. 1 dc) in next sc. 1 sc in top of next Shell. Pat to end of row. Turn.

7th row: Pat across to last sc. (1 dc. Ch 2. 1 dc) in last sc. 1 dc in top of turning ch 3. Turn.

Rep 4th to 7th rows 1 (**2**-2) time(s) more then 4th and 5th rows once. 3 shells.

Cont even in pat until armhole measures 7 (**7½**-8) ins [18 (**19**-20.5) cm], ending with RS facing for next row. Fasten off.

With RS of work facing, join yarn with sl st in same sp as last sc. Ch 1. 1 sc in same sp as last sl st. Pat to end of row. Turn.

2nd row: Pat to last sc. 2 dc in last sc. Turn.

3rd row: Ch 3 (counts as dc). Miss first 2 dc. (1 dc. Ch 2. 1 dc) in next sc. 1 sc in top of next Shell. Pat to end of row. Turn.

4th row: Pat to last sc. Shell in last sc. 1 dc in next ch-2 sp. Miss next dc. 1 dc in top of turning ch. Turn.

5th row: Ch 3 (counts as dc). 1 sc in top of next Shell. Pat to end of row. Turn.

6th row: Pat to last Shell. 1 sc in top of last Shell. (1 dc. Ch 2. 1 dc) in next sc. 1 dc in top of turning ch. Turn.

7th row: Ch 3 (counts as dc). (1 dc. Ch 2. 1 dc) in next sc. 1 sc in top of next Shell. Pat to end of row. Turn.

Rep 4th to 7th rows 1 (**2**-2) time(s) more then 4th and 5th rows once. 3 Shells.

Cont even in pat until armhole measures 7 (**7½**-8) ins [18 (**19**-20.5 cm], ending with RS facing for next row. Fasten off.

BACK

Work from ** to ** as given for Front.

Cont even in pat until armhole measures same length as Front to shoulders, ending with RS facing for next row. Fasten off.

SLEEVES

With smaller hook, ch 74 (**80**-86).

Foundation row: (RS). 1 sc in 2nd ch from hook. *Miss next 2 ch. Shell in next ch. Miss next 2 ch. 1 sc in next ch. Rep from * to end of row. 12 (**13**-14) Shells.

Work even in pat as given for Front for 9 more rows.

Shape top: Next row: (RS). Sl st in (first dc, ch-2 sp, dc, sc, dc, ch-2 sp and dc). Ch 1. 1 sc in same sp as last sl st. Pat to last Shell. Miss next dc and ch-2 sp. 1 sc in next dc. **Turn.** Leave rem sts unworked. 10 (**11**-12) Shells.

2nd row: Sl st in (first sc, dc, ch-2 sp and dc). Ch 1. 1 sc in same sp as last sl st. Pat to last Shell. Miss next dc and ch-2 sp. 1 sc in next dc. **Turn.** Leave rem sts unworked.

Rep last row until there are 2 (**3**-3) Shells. Fasten off.

INSTRUCTIONS CONT.

FINISHING

Sew shoulder seams.

Front or Back Bottom Edging: With RS of work facing and larger hook, join yarn with sl st in first rem loop of foundation ch. Ch 1. 1 sc in same sp as last sl st. *Miss next 2 ch. (3 dc. *Ch 3. Sl st to top of last dc* - Picot made. 2 dc) in next ch. Miss next ch. 1 sc in next ch. Rep from * to end of row. Fasten off.

Bottom Sleeve Edging: With smaller hook, work as given for Front or Back Bottom Edging.

Sew in Sleeves. Sew side and sleeve seams.

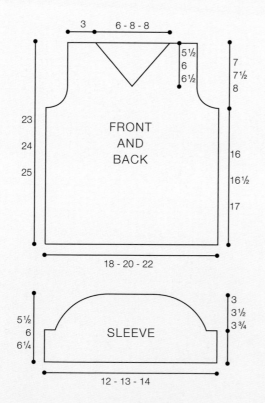

Floral Shawl

MEASUREMENT

Approx 26 ins [66 cm] wide x 70 ins [178 cm] long

MATERIALS

Patons Grace (50 g/1.75 oz)

60005 (Snow) 13 **balls**

Sizes 3.5 mm (U.S. E or 4) and 4.5 mm (U.S. 7) crochet hooks **or size needed to obtain tension.**

TENSION

2 flowers = 3½ ins [9.5 cm] wide with larger hook in pat.

INSTRUCTIONS

With larger hook, ch 135.

1st row: (RS). 2 dc in 4th ch from hook. Miss next 2 ch. Sl st in next ch. Ch 7. Miss next 3 ch. Sl st in next ch. *Ch 3. Miss next 2 ch. (Sl st. Ch 3. 2 dc. Ch 3. sl st) all in next ch. Ch 3. 2 dc in next ch. Miss next 2 ch. Sl st in next ch. Ch 7. Miss next 3 ch. Sl st in next ch. Rep from * to last 3 ch. Ch 3. Miss next 2 ch. (Sl st. Ch 3. 2 dc) all in last ch. (1st row of Chart is now complete, noting 11 ch repeat will be worked 11 times). **Do not turn.**

Note: Refer to Chart to follow instructions for remaining rows. **All** rows will be worked with RS facing. When working 2nd and 4th rows of pat, rotate Shawl so foundation row is at top of work.

2nd row: *Ch 10. Sl st in 4th ch from hook to form loop. Ch 3. 2 dc in loop. Sl st in ch-7 sp. Ch 3. (Sl st. Ch 3. 2 dc) in same loop. Ch 3. Sl st in top of ch 3 in row below. Rep from * across, ending with sl st in top of ch 3. **Do not turn.**

3rd row: Ch 9. *Sl st in top of dc. Ch 3. (Sl st. Ch 3. 2 dc. Ch 3. Sl st. Ch 3. 2 dc) all in loop. Sl st in 3rd ch from loop. Ch 7. Rep from * across, ending with ch 3. *(Yoh) 3 times and draw up a loop in dc. (Yoh and draw through 2 loops on hook) 4 times – dtr made.* **Do not turn.**

4th row: Ch 6. Sl st in 3rd ch from hook to form loop. Ch 3. 2 dc in loop. Ch 3. Sl st in top of ch 3. *Ch 10. Sl st in 4th ch from hook to form loop. Ch 3. 2 dc in loop. Sl st in ch-7 sp. Ch 3. (Sl st. Ch 3. 2 dc) in same loop. Ch 3. Sl st in top of ch 3. Rep from * across, ending with ch 10. Sl st in 4th ch from hook to form loop. Ch 3. 2 dc in loop. Sl st in 6th ch of turning ch. Ch 3. Sl st in loop. **Do not turn.**

CHART

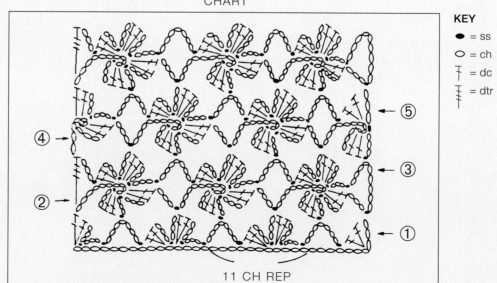

KEY

● = ss
○ = ch
┬ = dc
╪ = dtr

11 CH REP

5th row: Ch 3. 2 dc in loop. *Sl st in 3rd ch from loop. Ch 7. Sl st in top of dc. Ch 3. (Sl st. Ch 3. 2 dc. Ch 3. Sl st. Ch 3. 2 dc) all in loop. Rep from * across, ending with sl st in 4th ch from loop. Ch 7. Sl st in side of dc. Ch 3. (Sl st. Ch 3. 2 dc) all in loop. **Do not turn.**

Rep 2nd to 5th rows to form pat.

Cont in pat until work from beg measures approx 70 ins [178 cm], ending on a 4th row of pat. Fasten off.

Edging: 1st rnd: With RS of work facing and smaller hook, join yarn with sl st to any corner of Shawl. Work 1 row of sc evenly around outer edges, working 3 sc in corners. Join with sl st to first sc.

2nd rnd: **Ch 1.** 1 sc in each of first 3 sc. *Ch 3. *Sl st in last sc* – picot made. 1 sc in each of next 3 sc. Rep from * around. Join with sl st to first sc. Fasten off.

Easy Tank Top

SIZES

Bust measurement

Extra-Small   32 ins   [81   cm]
Small   34 "   [86   "]
Medium   36 "   [91.5 "]

Finished bust

Extra-Small   34 ins   [86   cm]
Small   36 "   [91.5 "]
Medium   38 "   [96.5 "]

MATERIALS

Patons Grace (50 g/1.75 oz)

	XS	S	M
60902 (Spearmint)	5	6	7 **balls**

Size 2.75 mm (U.S. C or 2) crochet hook **or size needed to obtain tension.**

TENSION

24 sts and 13 rows = 4 ins [10 cm] in pattern.

INSTRUCTIONS

The instructions are written for smallest size. If changes are necessary for larger sizes the instructions will be written thus ( ).

BACK

**Ch 106 (112-118).

1st row: (RS). 2 dc in 4th ch from hook. *Ch 1. Miss next 5 ch. 5 dc in next ch. Rep from * to last 6 ch. Ch 1. Miss next 5 ch. 3 dc in last ch. Turn.

2nd row: Ch 1. 1 sc in first dc. *Ch 2. Miss next 2 dc. *(1 dc. Ch 3. Sls t in top of last dc. 1 dc) in next ch-1 sp* – Picot V made. Ch 2. Miss next 2 dc. 1 sc in next dc. Rep from * ending last rep in top of turning ch. Turn.

3rd row: Ch 3 (counts as 1 dc). 2 dc in first sc. *Ch 1. 5 dc in next sc. Rep from * to last sc. Ch 1. 3 dc in last sc. Miss turning ch. Turn.

Rep 2nd and 3rd rows for pat.

Cont even in pat until work from beg measures 10 (10½-12) ins [25.5 (27-30.5) cm], ending with a 3rd row of pat.

Shape armhole: (WS). Sl st in each of first 12 sts. Ch 1. 1 sc in next dc. *Ch 2. Miss next 2 dc. Picot V in next ch-1 sp. Ch 2. Miss next 2 dc. 1 sc in next dc. Rep from * 12 (14-15) times more. Turn.**

Cont even in pat until work from beg measures 15 (15½-16½) ins [30 (39.5-42) cm], ending with a 3rd row of pat.

Neck shaping: ***Next row: (WS). Ch 1. 1 sc in first st. (Ch 2. Miss next 2 dc. Picot V in next ch-1 sp. Ch 2. Miss next 2 dc. 1 sc in next dc) twice. Turn. Cont even in pat over these 13 sts, until work from beg measures 17¼ (17¾-19¼) ins [44 (45.5-49) cm], ending with a 3rd row of pat. Fasten off.

With WS facing, miss next 55 (61-67) sts. Join yarn with sl st to next st. Ch 1. 1 sc in same sp as last sl st. (Ch 2. Miss next 2 dc. Picot V in next ch-1 sp. Ch 2. Miss next 2 dc. 1 sc in next dc) twice. Turn. Cont even in pat over these 13 sts, until work from beg measures 17¼ (17¾-19¼) ins [44 (45.5-49) cm], ending with a 3rd row of pat. Fasten off.***

FRONT

Work from ** to ** as given for Back.

Cont even in pat until work from beg measures 14 (14¼-15½) ins [35.5 (36-39.5) cm], ending with a 3rd row of pat.

Neck shaping: Work from *** to *** as given for Back.

Bottom Edging: With RS of Front facing, join yarn with sl st to first ch of foundation ch. Ch 3. 2 dc in same sp. *Ch 1. Miss next 5 ch. 5 dc in next ch. Rep from * across, working only 3 dc at end of last rep. Fasten off.

Rep for Back.

Finishing: Sew shoulder and side seams.

Neck Edging: With RS facing, join yarn with sl st to shoulder seam at neck edge. Ch 1. 1 sc in same sp. Work 1 row of sc evenly around neck edge. Join with sl st to first sc. Fasten off.

Armhole Edging: With RS facing, join yarn with sl st to armhole edge at side seam. Ch 1. 1 sc in same sp. Work 1 row of sc around armhole. Join with sl st to first sc. Fasten off.

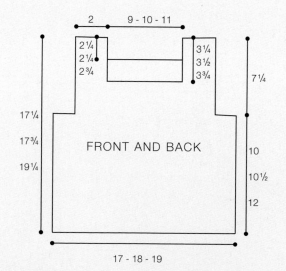

Pretty Twin Set

SIZES

Cardigan

Bust measurement

Small	34 ins	[86.5 cm]
Medium	36 "	[91.5 "]
Large	38 "	[96.5 "]

Finished bust measurement

Small	35 ins	[89 cm]
Medium	37 "	[94 "]
Large	39 "	[99 "]

Camisole

To fit bust measurement

Small	34 ins	[86.5 cm]
Medium	36 "	[91.5 "]
Large	38 "	[96.5 "]

MATERIALS

Patons Grace (50 g/1.75 oz)

Sizes	S	M	L	
Cardigan (60416 Blush)	9	10	10	**balls**
Camisole (60416 Blush)	4	4	4	**balls**

Size 3.5 mm (U.S. E or 4) crochet hook **or size needed to obtain tension**. 5 buttons for Cardigan. 5 buttons for Camisole.

TENSION

8½ V-sts and 14 rows = 4 ins [10 cm]

INSTRUCTIONS

The instructions are written for smallest size. If changes are necessary for larger sizes, the instructions will be written thus ( ).

Cardigan

BACK

Ch 111 (**117**-123).

**Foundation row: (RS). *(1 hdc. Ch 1. 1 hdc) all in 4th ch from hook* - V-st made. *Miss next 2 ch. V-st in next ch. Rep from * to last 2 ch. Miss next ch. 1 hdc in last ch. Turn.

Next row: Ch 2 (counts as first hdc). V-st in first V-st of previous row. V-st in each V-st to end of row. 1 hdc in top of turning ch 2. Turn. Last row forms pat.

Cont in pat until work from beg measures 11½ (**12½**-13½) ins [29 (**32**-34.5) cm], ending with RS facing for next row.**

Armhole shaping: 1st row: Ch 1. (1 sl st in next hdc, ch-1 sp, hdc) twice. Ch 2. V-st in each V-st to last 3 V-sts. 1 hdc in next V-st. **Turn.**

2nd row: Ch 2. 1 hdc in first V-st. V-st in each V-st to last 2 sts. *Yoh and draw up a loop in last hdc. Yoh and draw up a loop in top of turning ch. Yoh and draw through all loops on hook - hdc2tog made.* Turn.

Rep last row twice more.

Next row: (RS). Ch 2 (counts as first hdc). V-st in first V-st of previous row. V-st in each V-st to end of row. 1 hdc in top of turning ch 2. Turn. Rep last row 21 (**23**-23) times more. Fasten off.

LEFT FRONT

Ch 57 (**60**-63).

Rep from ** to ** as given for Back.

Armhole shaping: 1st row: (RS). Ch 1. (1 sl st in next hdc, ch-1 sp, hdc) twice. Ch 2. V-st in each V-st to end of row. 1 hdc in top of turning ch 2. Turn.

2nd row: Ch 2 (counts as first hdc). V-st in first V-st of previous row. V-st in each V-st to last 2 sts. Hdc2tog over last hdc and turning ch. Turn.

3rd row: Ch 2. 1 hdc in first V-st. V-st in each V-st to end of row. 1 hdc in top of turning ch 2. Turn.

4th row: Ch 2 (counts as first hdc). V-st in first V-st of previous row. V-st in each V-st to last 2 sts. Hdc2tog over last hdc and turning ch. Turn.

V-neck shaping: 1st row: (RS). Ch 2 (counts as first hdc). V-st in first V-st of previous row. V-st in each V-st to last V-st. Hdc2tog over ch-1 sp and turning ch. Turn.

2nd row: Ch 2 (counts as first hdc). V-st in first V-st of previous row. V-st in each V-st to end of row. 1 hdc in top of turning ch 2. Turn.

Rep last 2 rows 7 times more.

Next row: Ch 2 (counts as first hdc). V-st in first V-st of previous row. V-st in each V-st to end of row. 1 hdc in top of turning ch 2. Turn.

Rep last row 7 (**9**-9) times more. Fasten off.

RIGHT FRONT

Work as given for Left Front reversing **RS** rows for WS and **WS** rows for RS.

SLEEVES

Ch 60.

Foundation row: (RS). *(1 hdc. Ch 1. 1 hdc) all in 4th ch from hook* - V-st made. *Miss next 2 ch. V-st in next ch. Rep from * to last 2 ch. Miss next ch. 1 hdc in last ch. Turn. 19 V-sts.

Next row: Ch 2 (counts as first hdc). V-st in first V-st of previous row. V-st in each V-st to end of row. 1 hdc in top of turning ch 2. Turn.

Rep last row twice more.

Next row: Ch 2 (counts as first hdc). 1 hdc in first hdc. V-st in first V-st of previous row. V-st in each V-st to end of row. 2 hdc in top of turning ch 2. Turn.

Next row: Ch 2 (counts as first hdc). 1 hdc in first hdc. 1 hdc in next hdc. V-st in first V-st of previous row. V-st in each V-st to last 2 sts. 1 hdc in next hdc. 2 hdc in top of turning ch 2. Turn.

Next row: Ch 2 (counts as first hdc). V-st in next hdc. Miss next hdc. V-st in each V-st to last 3 sts. Miss next hdc. V-st in next hdc. 1 hdc in top of turning ch 2. Turn.

Next row: Ch 2 (counts as first hdc). V-st in first V-st of previous row. V-st in each V-st to end of row. 1 hdc in top of turning ch 2. Turn.

Rep last 4 rows 4 (**5**-6) times more. 29 (**31**-33) V-sts.

Next row: Ch 2 (counts as first hdc). V-st in first V-st of previous row. V-st in each V-st to end of row. 1 hdc in top of turning ch 2. Turn.

Rep last row 25 (**23**-19) times more.

Top shaping: 1st row: Ch 1. (1 sl st in next hdc, ch-1 sp, hdc) twice. Ch 2. V-st in each V-st to last 3 V-sts. 1 hdc in next V-st. **Turn.**

2nd row: Ch 2. 1 hdc in first V-st. V-st in each V-st to last V-st. 1 hdc in next V-st. **Turn.**

3rd row: Ch 2. 1 hdc in first V-st. V-st in each V-st to last 2 sts. Hdc2tog over last hdc and turning ch. Turn.

Rep last row 11 times more. Fasten off.

INSTRUCTIONS CONT.

FINISHING

Sew side and shoulder seams.

Edging: 1st rnd: With RS of work facing, join yarn with sl st to bottom corner of Right Front. Ch 1. 3 sc in same sp as last sl st. Work 64 (**69**-74) sc up Right Front to front shaping. 2 sc in next corner st. Work 34 (**36**-38) sc up Right Front V-neck shaping to shoulder. Work 34 sc across Back neck edge. Work 34 (**36**-38) sc down Left Front V-neck shaping. 2 sc in next corner st. Work 64 (**69**-74) sc down Left Front to bottom. 3 sc in next corner st. *1 sc in each of next 2 sts. Miss next st. Rep from * across bottom of Cardigan. Join with ss to first sc.

2nd rnd: Ch 1. 1 sc in same sp as last ss. 3 sc in next sc. 1 sc in each of next 2 (**1**-1) sc. [Ch 2 (for buttonhole). Miss next 2 sc. 1 sc in each of next 13 (**14**-15) sc] 4 times. Ch 2. Miss next 2 sc. 1 sc in each sc to V-neck shaping. 2 sc in next sc. 1 sc in each sc to Left Front V-neck shaping. 2 sc in next sc. 1 sc in each sc to bottom of Cardigan. 3 sc in next corner. 1 sc in each sc across bottom of Cardigan. Join with sl st to first sc.

3rd rnd: Ch 1. Working from **left** to right instead of from **right** to left, as usual, work 1 sc in each sc around for reverse sc. Join with sl st to first sc. Fasten off.

Sleeve Edging: Sew in sleeves. Sew side and sleeve seams.

1st rnd: With RS of work facing, join yarn with sl st at seam. *1 sc in each of next 2 sts. Miss next st. Rep from * around. Join with sl st to first sc.

2nd rnd: Ch 1. 1 sc in each sc around. Join with sl st to first sc.

3rd rnd: Ch 1. Working from **left** to right instead of from **right** to left, as usual, work 1 sc in each sc around for reverse sc. Join with sl st to first sc. Fasten off.

Sew buttons to correspond to buttonholes.

Camisole

BACK

Ch 105 (**111**-117).

**Foundation row: (RS). *(1 hdc. Ch 1. 1 hdc)* all in 4th ch from hook - V-st made. *Miss next 2 ch. V-st in next ch. Rep from * to last 2 ch. Miss next ch. 1 hdc in last ch. Turn.

Next row: Ch 2 (counts as first hdc). V-st in first V-st of previous row. V-st in each V-st to end of row. 1 hdc in top of turning ch 2. Turn.

Last row forms pat.

Cont in pat until work from beg measures 10 (**11**-12) ins [25.5 (**28**-30.5) cm] ending with WS facing for next row.** Fasten off.

LEFT FRONT

Ch 54 (**57**-60).

Rep from ** to ** as given for Back.

Front and armhole shaping: 1st row: Ch 2. 1 hdc in first V-st. V-st in each of next 13 (**14**-15) V-sts. 1 hdc in next V-st. **Turn.**

***2nd row: Ch 2. 1 hdc in first V-st. V-st in each V-st to last 2 sts. Hdc2tog over last hdc and turning ch. Turn.

Rep last row until "**Next row: 1 hdc. V-st. Hdc2tog over last hdc and turning ch**" has been worked.

Next row: Ch 2. 1 hdc in next V-st. Hdc2tog over last hdc and turning ch. Turn.

Next row: Ch 2. Miss first st. Hdc2tog over next hdc and turning ch. Fasten off. ***

RIGHT FRONT

Ch 54 (**57**-60).

Rep from ** to ** as given for Back.

Next row: Ch 1. (Sl st in next hdc, ch-1 sp, hdc) twice. Ch 2. 1 hdc in next V-st. V-st in each of next 13 (**14**-15) V-sts. 1 hdc in next V-st. 1 hdc in top of turning ch. Turn.

Rep from *** to *** as given for Left Front.

FINISHING

Sew side seams.

With RS of work facing, join yarn with sl st to bottom corner of Right Front.

1st rnd: Ch 1. 3 sc in corner st. Work 50 (**55**-60) sc up Right Front to front shaping. 2 sc in next corner st. Work 27 (**31**-35) sc up Right Front shaping. 5 sc in top st. Work 27 (**31**-35) sc down Right Front shaping. Work 8 (**16**-20) sc to side seam. Work 72 (**76**-82) sc across Back. Work 8 (**16**-20) sc from side seam to Left Front shaping. Work 37 sc up Left Front shaping. 5 sc in top st. Work 37 sc down Left Front shaping. Work 50 (**55**-60) sc down Left Front to bottom. Join with sl st to first sc.

2nd rnd: Ch 1. Work 1 sc in each sc along bottom of Right Front. 3 sc in corner sc. 1 sc in next 2 sc. [Ch 2. Miss next 2 sc. 1 sc in each of next 10 (**11**-12) sc] 4 times. 1 sc in each sc to first corner sc. 2 sc in corner sc. 1 sc in each sc to end of rnd, working 5 sc in top sc, 2 sc in front corner and 3 sc in bottom corners. Join with sl st to first sc.

INSTRUCTIONS CONT.

3rd rnd: Ch 1. Working from **left** to right instead of from **right** to left, as usual, work 1 sc in each sc around for reverse sc. Join with sl st to first sc (see diagram). Fasten off.

Straps: (make 2). **1st row:** Ch 4. 1 sc in 2nd ch from hook. 1 sc in each ch to end of row. Turn.

2nd row: Ch 1. 1 sc in each sc to end of row. Turn. Rep last row until work from beg measures 15 ins [38 cm]. Fasten off.

Sew Straps to Fronts at points. Try on Camisole and adjust straps to fit. Sew in position to Back. Sew buttons to correspond to buttonholes.

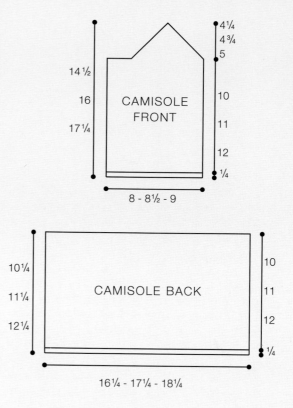

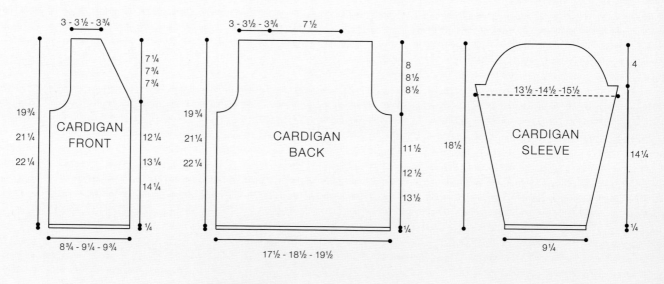

REVERSE SC

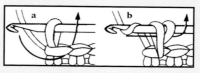

Resources

Patons Yarns

320 Livingstone Avenue South

Listowel, ON

Canada

N4W 3H3

www.patonsyarns.com

Acknowledgments

SPECIAL THANKS TO THE PATONS DESIGN TEAM:

Designers:

Svetlana Avraka

Zena Low

Kara Guild

Gayle Bunn

Fiona Ellis

Marketing Manager:

Sara Arblaster

Graphics:

Julie Le

Marketing Support:

Doris Erb

Kathy Hicks

Barb Ward

Leianne Gooding

Creative and Marketing Director:

Catherine N. Blythe